THE POWER IN LOGIC PRO

quickPRO
guides

THE POWER IN LOGIC PRO

Songwriting, Composing, Remixing, and Making Beats

Dot Bustelo

Hal Leonard Books
An Imprint of Hal Leonard Corporation

Published in 2012 by Hal Leonard Books
An Imprint of Hal Leonard Corporation
7777 West Bluemound Road
Milwaukee, WI 53213

Trade Book Division Editorial Offices
33 Plymouth St., Montclair, NJ 07042

Printed in United States of America

Book design by Adam Fulrath
Book composition by Kristina Rolander

Library of Congress Cataloging-in-Publication Data

Bustelo, Dot.
 The power in Logic Pro : songwriting, composing, remixing, and making beats / Dot Bustelo.
    p. cm.
1. Logic (Computer file) 2. Digital audio editors. I. Title.
  ML74.4.L64B87 2012
  781.3'4536--dc23

                                    2012002230

ISBN 978-1-4584-1419-9

www.halleonardbooks.com

Contents

Chapter 3

Chapter 6

Chapter 7

Chapter 8

Chapter 9

Chapter 10

Especially for Composers (and Arrangers in the Modern World) 117

Chapter 11

Good Housekeeping (and Other Smart Practices)......................131

Chapter 12

PREFACE

This book is based on the method of introducing Logic I developed while working with some of the greatest artists of our time during my years at Apple on the worldwide Logic team, and before that at Emagic. I had the privilege of demonstrating to musicians from all over the world at countless recording studios, homes, tradeshows, and music stores while I was on my own humble path to produce music and become one with Logic. This book is designed to get you over the initial hurdle of learning Logic that I'm happy to have helped so many musicians get past as quickly as possible. My hope is that once you're up and running, this book remains your studio guide as you continue to find energy and headspace to expand on your creative process in Logic. I have carefully selected the topics that world-touring bands, rock stars, hit producers, professional engineers, international DJs, aspiring musicians, and hobbyists have asked me time and again to explain. It's my pleasure to pass along a body of creative and technical knowledge that was shared with me by the incredibly passionate team of Logic developers and other former colleagues at Apple and Emagic, all of whom I genuinely consider my family.

Digital technology is making music production more and more accessible—so everyone can have a bedroom studio with the potential to sound great. But for most people, it remains a tease because there's no assurance that they'll really know what to do with it. A new user must get past that major hump at the beginning then make the effort to continue actively learning. Over time, the art of learning becomes incremental and very satisfying. Knowledge of a new feature can be as thrilling as a new piece of gear.

The best advice I have for becoming "one" with Logic is to treat it like an instrument, like learning to play the piano or the guitar. You have to learn the language of the instrument, and you have to practice. Give yourself focused, disciplined time—besides the time you plan to write in Logic—to learn your new instrument. Take the pressure off yourself of having to create a masterpiece each time you launch the app. You don't even have to feel inspired when you boot it up. Just poke around and start shopping for sounds in the vast collection of software instruments, plug-in settings, channel strip settings, and Apple Loops. Start saving your own folders of custom channel strip settings into the Library with Logic or third-party instruments, and Logic will start to become your own personal instrument. Build your own mega EXS24 sample library so your drum samples can easily be saved within your Logic project. You will develop your own unique sound within Logic, and when you learn which assets need to be backed up, you can carry your own Logic sounds everywhere, and load them into anyone's Logic studio. (See chapter 7, "Creating with Logic's Software Instruments," and chapter 11, "Good Housekeeping and Other Smart Practices.")

Time needs to be spent learning Logic, practicing the tools and navigation. Above all, to learn the language of Logic, study the key command shortcuts. When I was learning Logic, I got the advice from more senior Emagic colleagues to print these out and hang them in my bathroom. I didn't exactly do that, but I did carry them around with me. I printed them out using a little trick in the Key Commands window (under Options > Copy Key Commands to Clipboard), then dropped this into Microsoft Word and—bam!—ready to print. (See chapter 6, "The Secret to Learning Logic Key Commands," for details.)

No, I never learned every key command, but I do have a "hot list" of my favorite 30 key commands that I share in Appendix A of this book. Study these, cross-reference any unfamiliar terminology in the Help files, then make your own set of power key commands for your workflow, and you're on the path to becoming one with Logic.

The reputation that Logic sounds better and grooves better than other DAWs is a significant legacy from the Emagic days, and there are reasons for both these truisms that will be covered throughout this QuickPro book series.

I'm also honored to introduce two extremely prominent Logic users—Jay Z's engineer, Young Guru, and Mat Mitchell, whose credits include engineer/musician and technical genius for Tool, NIN, and Katy Perry, to name a few—who share a few of their favorite techniques for making music groove better in Logic. You'll find their advice mainly in chapter 9, where beat-making tools are featured, so bear with the methodology of this book to prepare yourself for their favorite tools. Both engineers coincidentally say they learned Logic by reading the manual, so consider yourself in good company for making time to read about your tools.

Methodology for This Book

Though the chapters are logically sequenced to read in a linear fashion, the information in each is self-contained and so can be read on its own.

In a perfect world you could inject all the information of the book simultaneously. But until we can jack into the matrix, read this book in any sequence you like—in whatever way you're inspired to use it.

Sometimes there will be a "To Do" summary at the top of a chapter or section that will be explained in more detail in the text that follows it. You'll also find QuickTime movies on the accompanying DVD-ROM that further illustrate certain points, and I encourage you to watch them as well so that you can see the tools and tricks in action. You should follow along, then write your own track using the tools.

Some features and exercises require Logic 9 or above.

ACKNOWLEDGMENTS

To my Emagic and Apple family who have freely shared their knowledge and their passion for Logic with me through the years: Bob Hunt, Bill Lee, Brian Miller, Clint Ward, Doug Roberts, Andrew Finley, Rick Moisan, Byron Gaither, Manfred Knaupp, Gorden Keppel, Thorsten Adams, Gerhard Lengeling, Sven Junge, Jeff Taylor, Stephen Gehring, and Steffan Diedrichsen. May the spirit of Emagic live on.

With equal gratitude to the countless artists whose insatiable desire for a mastery of Logic has driven me further into an exploration of Logic's creative potential than I could have imagined. Especially to the artists and friends who directly helped with this book on such short notice: Mat Mitchell, Young Guru, James Valentine, Jesse Carmichael, Ronnie Vannucci, Dave Darlington, Mark "Exit" Goodchild, Rick Sheppard, Empress, Nathaniel Motte, Jeff Allison, Chad Hugo, Ryan Tedder, A-trak, Phil Tan, Monica Tannian, Beth Sheppard, and James McKinney. The depth of all of your vision and focus has been daily inspiration; your friendship is my honor and privilege.

To my family for all their love and support, and to my developmental editor, Bill Gibson, for always getting it and me. To my singer, my music partner, and my muse, Cica, and to our music, Perfect Project, that would not exist without Logic and that I would not exist without.

To the continued evolution of music through new technology. May it continue to inspire all of us to express the rhythm and the soul of life in new ways.

THE POWER IN LOGIC PRO

Introduction
BECOMING ONE WITH LOGIC

I'll start at the beginning of my journey to the center of Logic. I moved to New York from Boston with my band, my Roland Juno-106 keyboard, and my Roland MC-50mkII sequencer in the mid-'90s. Desktop computers were already in the studio, but I didn't like them. I thought they belonged in the office, not the studio.

Gradually, I started using a Power Mac with Opcode Studio Vision software that the drummer bought, and I got a job selling keyboards and drum machines on 48th Street at Manny's Music store. It was still the place to buy gear in New York, and you never knew who was going to walk into the store at any time. It was located next to the biggest Sam Ash store in the country before Guitar Center arrived in Manhattan, and the street corner was a serious gathering place for pro musicians to exchange knowledge and hang. Sales guys were amped up and knew about every new piece of gear that came into the store. This was the '90s, and there were tons of studio rooms going up and no YouTube videos to learn how to do anything. Musicians and producers needed knowledgeable sales guys, and it was an honor to become one myself.

The greatest irony for me about getting a job in a music store was that music stores intimidated me even though I was a bit of a nerd. I assumed that it was because of my gender, which happens to be female. But a funny thing started happening. Customers were coming to me for help. I quietly started going into the store early, reading the manuals, and signing gear out at night to learn at home. I began noticing something else a bit odd: how a lot of guys who came into the store had no clue what they were talking about. They were asking me what MIDI was, what kind of cables they needed, and whether we carried a MIDI to audio cable!

My confidence grew with my awareness of their need for information. I realized that gear is confusing to everyone. What we all share is at one point having to jump in—and that the beginning is the worst when you have a minimal foundation in the language of the studio itself or in computer-based recording.

Meanwhile, Studio Vision was crashing a lot, especially with audio. The hip-hop guys and the geeks in the Manny's Music pro audio department told me to go with

Logic—that it was dope and that if I wanted to get paid in New York, I should learn Logic. That Pro Tools users were a dime a dozen, but if I learned Logic, I'd be special. Logic was deeper, more flexible, and you could just do more with it. I'd be able to support the serious composers and producers in New York. So I got Logic.

Then something life changing happened. This extremely cool rep from Emagic, Rick Moisan, walked into the store one day and took a few of us salespeople out to dinner. A year later he was promoted to COO of Emagic Inc., the U.S. distributor of Emagic GmbH, and tracked me down to apply for his old position. Some friends told me not to do it because it would kill my career as an artist and producer. Well, I went for it.

I then embarked on the best two years of my professional life, repping Logic. Emagic was hands down the coolest company I've ever worked for, and most everyone else who worked there would say the same thing. It was a perfect culture built around a highly creative music tool that was extremely profitable—software has pretty low manufacturing costs after all, once the product is designed. And we were living at that unique time in history when music software was coming into its own at an accelerated rate, largely due to the new speed of computers. Emagic was becoming a pioneer in developing virtual instruments, and they were working flawlessly in Logic. Everyone at the company was a pro, completely unique, maybe a bit eccentric, but we were all passionate about Logic. We'd get together at trade shows and nerd out in each other's hotel rooms until the wee hours sharing Logic tricks, complaining among ourselves about Logic's embarrassing shortcomings. The German programmers and all of us reps were "one"—it was a true global circle of creative knowledge.

Visiting music stores was admittedly challenging. Logic was still the underdog compared with Pro Tools, and Digital Performer and Cubase were still major players in the game. I'd go into music stores in New Jersey or Maryland, and there'd be only one sales guy doing electronic music who was excited that I was coming. The rest were indifferent. They thought Logic was too complicated and had too steep a learning curve, which to me was very shortsighted. How could you pass up free knowledge in the general field you are interested in when it's walking in the door? Who's to say how hard the best software in the world should be to learn, anyway?

Myself, I was blind to the learning curve in Logic. As long as I knew how to load sounds, record, quantize, and delete, I was good. Sure, there were frustrations when the audio was fighting me with distortion, low signal levels, or freezing with cryptic error messages. I learned to keep a log of what I was doing when the train wreck occurred and take a screen shot to report the exact error message. I'd control the aggravation that "I had no time for this!" and run the drill of checking the signal path, swapping out cables, rechecking settings in the software, downloading new drivers, restarting the computer and trashing Logic prefs, all the usual suspects. The idea was simply to never give up when things aren't working. We are still smarter than the machines, so figure it out or find a workaround as a temporary solution. As my friend and Grammy-winning engineer Dave Darlington always says, "Machines don't win. People do!"

One Monday morning we woke up to the news on the Emagic homepage that Apple had bought our company. I stood up, put the Sony PC that Emagic had recently sent me in the closet, and happily streamlined my studio. Logic was ironically rocking on a PC in version 5, but ultimately the acquisition was the best thing that could have happened to the program. Its interface and workflow became "Apple-ized"—cleaner, simpler, and more intuitive.

Still to this day there remains beneath the surface the profound tools that gave Logic its enduring personality and depth as the most powerful creative tool on the planet. Nothing was removed from the toolkit of Logic; even the dirty little secret of the Logic environment is still there with all its glorious intricacy of possibilities. Now Logic lives in the best of both worlds: the old-school flexibility and creativity, with the new-school Apple cleanliness of tools and efficient workflow. Tools were thankfully brought to the surface with features like the customizable toolbar and transport, contextual menus accessed by Ctrl-clicking (right-clicking) all over the screen, the dual channel strip, and the powerful Media area with the Settings Library, Browser, Bin, and Apple Loops.

A few years later I was promoted to the Worldwide Product Marketing team at Apple. We were responsible for the professional apps of Logic and Final Cut. It was an honor visiting the top studios in the country, the soundchecks, and homes of some of the greatest recording artists, producers, and engineers of our time. Whatever their musical genre or personal style, if they were at the top of their game, I found that they shared a remarkable ability to focus, to block out the entourage of people in the room or the concert looming in an arena in an hour, or in 15 minutes. They would stop and focus on the Logic screen to absorb knowledge. I remember T-Pain telling me to meet him in the studio after his headlining concert at Boston Garden. He was heading straight to the studio to work, not to an after-party. It's easy to criticize the music industry machine, but the truth is that most stars aren't stars by accident. They know how to focus on their craft.

Meanwhile, the tipping point was crossed for Logic. The credibility of Logic steadily began rising. The interface was improving so Logic was becoming more and more powerful and intuitive. Another belief was undeniable: if Apple owned Logic, it would over time perform really well on a Mac. No longer did I walk into a studio (let alone a music store) and have to defend Logic or why someone should even look at it. Suddenly I'd walk into the room and people were waiting for me. Producers, musicians, and even engineers wanted to learn as much as possible about Logic! As my good friend, engineer Mark "Exit" Goodchild (who at the time worked for Akon) said, "All the producers I work for use Logic, and I need to know more than they do about it so the session can go smoothly"—a forward-thinking perspective for the modern engineer accustomed to a Pro Tools–dominated studio environment. This was the beginning of the new era for Logic, where I was welcomed by top recording engineers.

When I sit down with new and not-so-new but still-confused Logic users, I always try to convey what I learned early on in my Emagic days. First of all, just use the program, a lot. Try to use it daily so that you can't help but become at ease with it. But really, a key to becoming "one" with Logic is to learn the language of Logic. It has its own vocabulary. Some of it is unique to Logic and a bit quirky, like the Transform window and the Hyper Editor. Other terms are shared with other applications within and outside the Apple universe, like the Marquee tool and the Inspector. The more you tune in to the vocabulary, the easier it will be for you to address a problem within Logic by using the Help files, learning from other Logic users, or Googling online a solution.

Just remember Logic is your instrument, your creative tool. Allow yourself the time to practice and learn it, then follow your own rules. It's a path of musical knowledge that I hope will inspire you as much as it has inspired me.

Chapter 1
SETTING UP YOUR LOGIC STUDIO

The Logic Help files do a great job of walking you through getting started, so this chapter will present only a quick lay of the land and a checklist of a few "gotcha's" when setting up your Logic studio.

Preparing to Launch

Installing Logic Studio will take a while if you install everything, which is both the blessing and the curse of all the incredible content that comes with Logic. The good news is that you don't have to install everything right away. After you enter your name and serial number using the main installer screen, you will see the option to disable the checkbox next to any components of the content that you don't need or don't have physical hard-drive space for. You can always go back and do a custom install to add this additional content that you omitted the first time, whether it consists of Apple Loops, Space Designer reverb content, and so on.

Custom Install and Changing the Install Location

The window where you make install selections is called the Custom Install pane.

Some of the content, including the Apple Loops, allows you to choose a custom location under the appropriately labeled Location column. Here's where you can choose between the internal boot drive and the secondary or external drives.

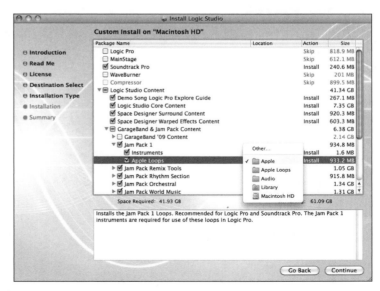

Changing the install path in the Custom Install pane

Saving Disk Space

If you skip the Apple Loops and other nonessential content, the main Logic application and factory EXS24 and Ultrabeat content is under 3GB. You can load the main application and factory presets in just minutes. If you are trying to save time or disk space, you may want to install only some of the included Apple Loop libraries.

Software Updates for Logic

Be sure to go to Software Update and run any updates to Logic after you install the application. These subreleases fix minor bugs and improve operation 99.97 percent of the time.

Performing an update on Logic is very different than making what should be a careful decision to upgrade your operating system. Update your operating system only after you check manufacturer websites and forums to be sure that all your third-party plug-ins and external hardware will be compatible.

Connecting External Audio

One way or the other, you have to input sound into Logic. It's either going to be audio or MIDI, so you'll have to configure some external hardware. Let's start with audio.

Down and Dirty with Built-In Sound

You have a choice when it comes to audio. You can connect an audio interface, which will allow you to plug in external mics and mic pres, as well as record at professional sample rates and bit depths. The interface converts the analog signal to a digital one that your computer and Logic can understand. Or, you can work down and dirty using the built-in sound output and even the built-in microphone on the Mac to do any recording in Logic in a pinch. Any audio recorded in this fashion will be only 44.1 kHz and 16-bit—consumer-level audio quality. If you're using a laptop, this can be convenient when you're on the go or just getting started with Logic and want to experiment with the software before making any investment in external hardware.

Built-in sound is easy. There are no drivers to install and no hardware to connect. Plug in your headphones, use the Mac's built-in speakers or the mini jack out of the Mac to your speakers. If you've already been using iTunes on the computer, Logic will default to outputting through those same speakers as soon as you load or record any audio.

You can confirm that Logic will utilize Built-In Sound by opening Logic's Audio Preferences. Select Preferences in the upper left toolbar area, and then select Audio (Preferences > Audio). Under Output Device, the default should be Built-in Output. Under Input Device, select Built-in Line Input. If you choose Built-In Mic, be aware that you may experience feedback. In the lower right of this Audio Preferences window, select Apply Changes.

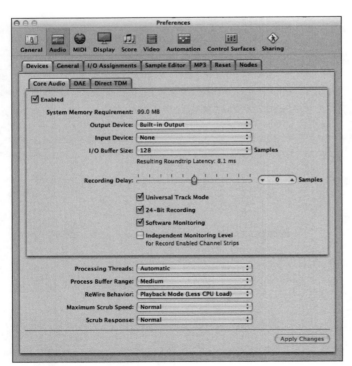

Audio preferences in Logic

Audio Drivers for External Hardware

When you're ready to step things up and use an audio interface with Logic, you will likely be connecting the device via USB, FireWire, PCI, or now Thunderbolt.

The first thing to do when you plug in the interface is to see if it's showing up. If it doesn't, then you'll have to install a driver. See the manufacturer's website for details.

Apple has made things a lot easier for manufacturers since OS X by creating what's called class-compliant Core Audio and MIDI drivers. These are drivers written by Apple that work with the current operating system, whether Snow Leopard, Lion, and so on. This means that a manufacturer doesn't have to write its own driver, which in the past varied in quality.

Sometimes the Core Audio driver will work for basic driving of inputting and outputting sound, but you'll still want the one written by the manufacturer for more advanced features to work. Don't bother using the driver that came on CD in the box with the audio interface. A newer and better one will likely be available on the manufacturer's website that will be more stable and feature-rich.

What is a *driver*, anyway? It is a tiny application that allows external hardware to speak to a computer. The quality of the driver is everything. Even if the manufacturer is well respected, do not immediately trust its brand-new audio interface. If it's released too early with a bad driver, you will have constant headaches such as error messages, latency issues, pops, and crackling sounds, all the way to no sound or sound cutting out. This is one of the most overlooked areas in evaluating the purchase of newly released hardware, and worth investigating other users' experiences on forums online.

Be careful, it can be confusing navigating manufacturer websites. Often Logic users contact me when a new interface isn't working, only to realize that they misread the driver list or install instructions. There is generally an exact procedure to follow (for example, whether the external hardware should be plugged in before or after the installation) in the Readme file Before You Install. The Readme file looks boring, but read it anyway. Always restart your computer after installing; think of it like flushing, if that helps you remember to do it.

Communicating with MIDI

If you're planning to create music by triggering any of the software instruments that come inside Logic, simply plug in a MIDI controller keyboard via USB, and it's plug and play (meaning it works right away). You plug it in, and then you play. If it doesn't instantly work, check the manufacturer's website for an updated driver, just as with your external audio hardware.

Loading a Software Instrument

Once the MIDI driver is installed, the easiest way to test it in Logic is to load a software instrument and try to play it. Loading a software instrument is covered in more detail in chapter 3, "Writing Your First Track in Logic." In summary, you will need to create a Software Instrument track first. Simply select the "+" on top of the Track List to launch the New Track dialog box and select Software Instrument. Logic will default to loading an electric piano that you can use to test your controller keyboard.

The MIDI Activity Monitor in Transport

If you don't hear any sound, check the MIDI Activity monitor in the Logic transport. The words "No In No Out" should switch to display the respective musical note on your keyboard (for example, C2, F4), with a number to the right indicating the velocity when you trigger MIDI from your keyboard. These values are to the right of the time signature, which will default to 4/4. If you don't see any activity in the Logic transport, the problem might not be with the controller's communication with Logic, but rather globally with the computer. Something may have gone wrong when installing the driver.

The MIDI Activity monitor in transport

The Audio MIDI Setup Utility

Your best tool for troubleshooting audio and MIDI issues is the Audio MIDI Setup utility (Applications > Utilities > Audio MIDI Setup Utility). I reference this tool so often that I recommend you drag it to your Dock.

The Audio MIDI Setup (AMS) utility

Within the utility, from the Window menu on top, select Show MIDI Window (Window > Show MIDI Window). Your keyboard controller should be visible in the MIDI window, and not grayed out.

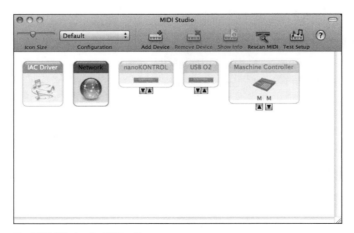

The MIDI Window in AMS utility

If your keyboard is not visible, select Re-Scan MIDI and try replugging in the physical USB cable between the controller and the computer again. When it's visible but grayed out, that can be an indication that the driver has been properly installed but the keyboard is not fully plugged in (for example, the cable could be loose, and so on).

Connecting Hardware Instruments

Hardware instruments, including keyboards and drum machines, are absolutely worth the effort to integrate into your Logic studio and make a powerful addition to your sound palette. You will need to connect the analog outputs for audio and set up a MIDI interface that connects via USB to your computer. MIDI cables will run from the keyboard or drum machine in both directions to the same port number on the MIDI interface (for example, Juno 106 MIDI Out to MIDI In Port 1 on your MIDI interface, Juno 106 MIDI In to MIDI Out Port 1 on the MIDI interface, and so on).

The trickiest part involves setting up Logic to recognize and recall the patch on your external hardware keyboard when you launch the Logic project the next time. See chapter 11, "Good Housekeeping and Other Smart Practices," for the steps to integrate the program names of any hardware keyboards.

Adding Third-Party Software Instruments

As amazing as the software instruments are that come with Logic, there is no reason not to expand your palette with third-party software instruments that will complement the sounds included with Logic. Software instruments or effects plug-ins (reverbs, EQs) that have worked inside the Logic application since OS X are referred to as Audio Units (AU), the plug-in architecture developed by Apple Inc.

The Audio Units Manager

After you install any third-party software instruments or effects plug-ins, you may need to launch the Audio Units Manager in Logic before they will be recognized (Preferences >Audio Units Manager). Depending on the plug-in, Logic may hang quite a bit on its startup screen before even launching. The Logic Preferences are located in the upper left of the toolbar. Once the Audio Units Manager is launched, locate the third-party instrument in question on the list and make sure that its checkbox is enabled in the left column.

If the Audio Unit wasn't immediately recognized, select Reset & Rescan Selection at the bottom. That will generally do the trick for any stubborn third-party software instrument or effects plug-in. Check the Logic Help files for more details.

Chapter 2
A FIVE-MINUTE TOUR OF THE ARRANGE WINDOW

This chapter is intentionally short. One mistake that new users make when I introduce them to Logic is to continually point to objects and icons in the workspace and ask, "What's that for?" When you are starting out, approach Logic on a need-to-know basis or else you will get distracted by its vastness. Follow this mini tour, and you'll know all you need to start driving.

Here is the brief setup you will need to do to take the tour:

To Do:

- Launch Logic.
- Select File > New.
- In the Templates dialog box, choose Select Empty Project.
- Select New Track dialog box in Arrange > Create 1 Audio Track.

Introducing the Arrange Window

Logic has been simplified to a one-window workspace called the Arrange window. There are many other powerful editors and windows in Logic that are optimized for different tasks, but you will likely spend the majority of your time using the Arrange window.

Every Logic project must have at least one track, so it makes sense that the first thing Logic will always do is to ask how many and what type of tracks you want when starting a new project. Choose one track for now, as directed in the To Do summary above. You are now looking at the Arrange window, the main window in Logic. If you are creating music in Logic, you really will spend most of your time here. Newer Logic users may not know this name for the window, but it's good to be aware of, especially if you're checking anything in the Help files.

The track list

Vertical Zoom

Understanding the Track List and Track Header

The track list is on your left. It includes audio tracks on which you record live audio, such as vocals and guitars, as well as audio files dragged in or otherwise imported from your hard drive. Also in the track list are the instrument tracks where you either play virtual instruments (called *software instruments* in Logic) or external MIDI instruments like a Korg Triton or Yamaha Motif keyboard.

If you Ctrl-click on the track name (labeled by default as Track 1, Track 2, Track 3, and so on), a contextual menu opens for configuring the track header. Here you can select which elements (such as Mute, Solo, Record Enable, Track Icons, and so on) will be in view on the track list.

Don't get lost in here now. It's enough just to know that it is there and that in the main Logic workspace, Ctrl-clicking on many objects will open contextual menus with tools that were once buried deep beneath the surface of Logic.

The vertical zoom can be adjusted with the vertical slider on the lower right of the window. Move the slider up and down to see the track size expand and compress.

You can always create more tracks with the "+" sign directly above the track list, in the global tracks header area.

Configure track header

The Transport

Beneath the main workspace is the transport. It is customizable by Ctrl-clicking in any part of the gray space to the left or right of the Transport buttons. The dialog box Customize Transport bar pops up, and a full-page sheet of options drops down with useful buttons and controls that you can add to the transport. You'll want to spend some time exploring your options here.

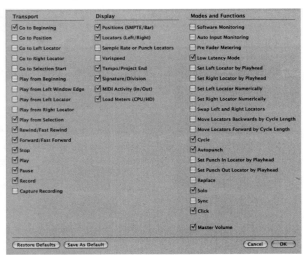

Customize Transport

A lot of those Transport buttons represent features that were accessible only as keyboard shortcuts (called "key commands" in the past). Under Apple's GUI guidance and direction, they are now brought to the surface and are available to add to the transport if desired for your workflow. One of my favorites is the Transport button called Capture Last Take, a key command I can't work without. This feature will be covered in the next chapter when we begin writing.

The Media Area: Apple Loops, Audio Bin, Library, and Browser

The right side of the Arrange window is a very rich design feature of Logic. Pro Tools users are familiar with an audio bin on the right side of the screen. Logic puts this idea on steroids, with it being a vast section called the Media area, which gives you access to the following:

- Bin: All the audio files recorded or imported to the current project
- Loops: A vast collection of audio and MIDI Apple Loops with metadata to conform to the tempo and key of your project
- Library: Software instrument or audio channel strip settings layered with effects plug-ins—an essential concept in Logic
- Browser: The navigation to all files on your Mac and connected hard drives from within Logic

Take a minute now to select these various tabs—Bin, Loops, Library, and Browser—to get a feel for the rich content that you have direct access to inside Logic.

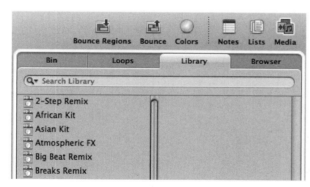

Media Tabs: Bin, Loops, Library, and Browser

The Bar Ruler, Toolbar, and Tool Menus

The upper portion of the Arrange window is dense with navigation and editing tools accessed in the bar ruler, toolbar, and Tool menus.

The Bar Ruler, Setting a Cycle Area

The bar ruler is your guide to the timeline in Logic and is always visible across the top of the Arrange window displaying bars and beats. Double-click in the lower half of the bar ruler to start playback from that location.

The bar ruler is also used to set up a cycle so that you can work on a specific section of your song. You select the cycle length by dragging in the upper half of the bar ruler. Let's set it to eight bars.

We need an Apple Loop in the workspace to continue our tour. Select Loops in the Media area to the right, and then click on any tab of your choice (Electric, Distorted, Horns, Bass, and so on). A list of loops will appear below. Click on any one that catches your fancy, and then drag it to the left into the main workspace on track 1. The loop will be shaded while it's selected. Now slide it over to bar 1 by watching both the bar ruler and the info line that pops up next to the Apple Loop as you're dragging.

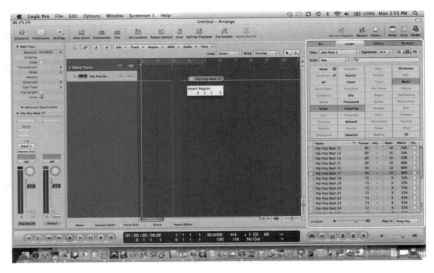

The bar ruler and info line on Apple Loop

Since the Logic project is still empty, a dialog box should pop up when you begin dragging the Apple Loop, asking if you want to import tempo information. Say yes for now.

Import tempo from Apple Loop

Logic's tempo, visible in the transport (top row, center), will conform to the default tempo of the Apple Loop.

Tempo in transport

Creating a Cycle or Region Loop

It will be helpful for this Apple Loop to play continuously, so let's set up a cycle. Click in the Apple Loop region so that it's highlighted, then select Set Locators in the toolbar area above the bar ruler.

You'll notice that a green bar in the bar ruler is now set to the same length as the Apple Loop. If you hit the Spacebar, the track will start playing and will cycle around the Apple Loop, going back to the top each time after it finishes playing back the loop. The toggle for enabling and disabling the cycle area is the button in the transport at the bottom right, with the two curved arrows forming a circle.

Set Locators tool; bar ruler display of Set Locators

Region Name and Region Header

There is visual feedback of whichever region you have highlighted. The region name located at the top of the region area called the Region Header will become shaded.

Congratulations! You've officially begun creating in Logic. But let's finish the tour now that we have some content in the workspace area of the Arrange window.

The Toolbar Is Cool and Customizable

The toolbar above the bar ruler has many great tools for navigating in Logic. If you Ctrl-click in the empty gray space, another sheet pulls down (just as is did in the transport area) of more tools you can add to the toolbar. Drag a tool to the toolbar to add it. Feel free to explore for a minute.

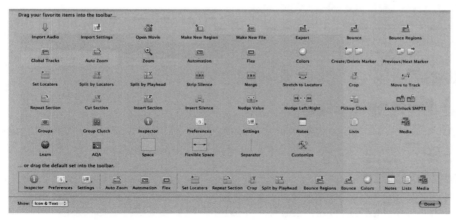

Customizing the toolbar

The Tool Menus

In the upper right of the Arrange window, just above the bar ruler but beneath the toolbar, are two small boxes that comprise the Tool menus. This is where you assign

Tool menus

your primary tool (left), and your alternate tool (right). When you click on the tool that's visible, a drop-down menu appears with all the other tools you can assign. The alternate tool is accessed when you hold down the Apple/Command key (right-click).

Primary Tool Assignment

The tool assignment in the Tool menus to the left defaults to the Pointer tool, which is likely what you will want it to be in the Arrange window and when using the other Editors. The symbol for the Pointer tool is the upward-pointing arrow. You can always use this menu to briefly reassign your primary tool, and then reassign the Pointer tool when you've finished a task.

Command-Click Tool Assignment

The box to the right should be assigned to whatever tool you use next often, second only to the Pointer tool. This tool will be accessed whenever you hold down the Apple/Command modifier key. Using an alternate tool is an extremely familiar workflow for any serious Logic user.

Power Tip: The Marquee Tool as a Command-Click Tool

The Marquee tool is the alternate tool of choice for power Logic users. It should be your main editing tool, because it is the most versatile. It is a relatively modern addition to the Logic tool palette. Its usefulness increases with every new version of the application, with dozens of tricks for navigation, editing, and even automation that will speed up your workflow (see chapter 5, "Navigating and Editing Made Simple," for a complete tour of the Marquee tool.

The Marquee tool as the Command-Click tool

Independent Tool Menus in Every Editor

You will find independently assignable Tool menus in not only the Arrange window but also all the other editors (Mixer, Piano Roll, and so on), which will be introduced below. Every editor has a main tool and an alternate tool accessed from the Apple/Command key. Familiarize yourself with the tools that are available as the alternate tool assignment in each editor to accommodate your workflow.

Power Tip: Third Tool Menu

Of special interest (especially to former PC users), a third tool can be assigned to right-clicking under Preferences > General > Editing > Right Mouse Button.

Essentials of the Mixer and Other Editors

The area below the Arrange area contains all the editors that you'll use when making more precise edits to your MIDI and audio as well as various adjustments to the mix.

Selecting Editors

By clicking on the tabs located beneath the Arrange window's workspace—Mixer, Piano Roll, Sample Editor, Score, and Hyper Editor—you can access the core editors in Logic that you will most often need besides the main Arrange window.

| Mixer | Sample Editor | Piano Roll | Score | Hyper Editor |

Selecting Editor tabs

Resizing the Editors

When you open an Edit window, you can click in the thin, gray empty space between that editor and the Arrange window to resize. A crosshair tool appears when you have found the sweet spot for making this adjustment.

Dual Channel Strip, Channel Strip Settings, and the Inspector

The dual channel strips and channel strip settings in the Inspector area are some of your greatest resources as a musician for creating your own unique sonic palette, with the sound of the professional engineer. Once you fully grasp the power of loading and saving software instruments, effects plug-ins, and sends in this area of the Arrange window, you will be extremely far along on your path with Logic. When you do have the opportunity to have a professional engineer visit your studio, you may want him or her to tweak some of the channel strip settings whether for your own vocals, guitar sound or software instruments, then save them in the Library for your future use.

Dual Channel Strip

You may have wondered why there are two mixer faders referred to as "channel strips" on the far left. This is an ingenious invention by the Logic developers that has nothing to do with mirroring a real-world mixer or console. There is no "two-channel" hardware mixer that this is emulating, but the idea is quite simple—to offer a way to work quickly while working creatively.

The channel strip on the left is the mixer channel for whatever track is highlighted in the Arrange window. You can adjust its volume and pan, and add effects plug-ins without having to go to the full Mixer view—right while recording or programming.

The channel strip to its right displays whatever the highlighted track in the track list (the leftmost channel strip) is sending signal to. By default it shows the main stereo output. However, it will update to show whatever the leftmost track is sending signal to via its sends, such as an auxiliary track.

With this dual channel strip design, you can monitor your signal flow and work quickly without needing to switch to the Mixer view. This means that you can practice proper gain structure like a professional engineer without even needing to open the Mixer. This way you can pay attention to whether any level changes or effects plug-ins introduced to an individual track are overloading the main output. This is the default use of Logic's dual channel strip.

It gets a lot more interesting when you start adding auxiliary tracks on the sends. Go ahead and click on the pane right beneath the label Sends on the leftmost channel strip.

Select Bus from the pull-down menu. Next, from the menu that opens, select Bus 1. While you do so, watch the transformation of the channel strip on the right closely. It is

Dual Channel Strip view: left to right, selected track, Stereo Output

no longer the Stereo Output. It becomes the first available auxiliary track to which you can now add an effects plug-in, whether a reverb, a delay, or some other type.

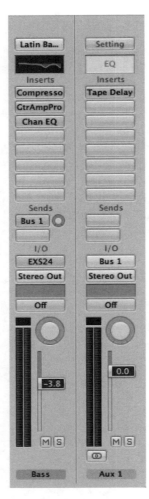

Auxiliary track creation

Stereo Outs in the Arrange window

To restore the channel strip on the right to displaying the main outputs, simply click on Stereo Out on the leftmost channel strip representing track 1 (or whichever track is highlighted in the track list).

Clever, right? With the dual channel strip design, you can stay in your writing and composing headspace with your linear arrangement in full view in the Arrange window, and throw on your "engineering cap" to sweeten the sound and control your gain structure.

Channel Strip Settings

A channel strip setting contains the entire routing configuration of a single channel strip, including all loaded plug-ins and settings, and can be created for an audio or a software instrument track.

You can save or load these settings by clicking on the Setting menu at the top of any channel. This will be discussed often throughout the book as an integral part of turning Logic into your instrument.

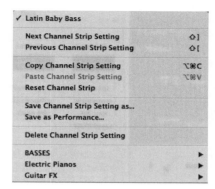

✓ Latin Baby Bass	
Next Channel Strip Setting	⇧]
Previous Channel Strip Setting	⇧[
Copy Channel Strip Setting	⌥⌘C
Paste Channel Strip Setting	⌥⌘V
Reset Channel Strip	
Save Channel Strip Setting as...	
Save as Performance...	
Delete Channel Strip Setting	
BASSES	▶
Electric Pianos	▶
Guitar FX	▶

Create Channel Strip Setting

The Inspector

The dual channel strip is actually part of a larger and very significant design feature of the Arrange window. The entire left-hand column is called the Inspector.

The Inspector can be toggled open or collapsed by clicking on the icon (which has a blue circle and the letter "I" in the center) that's at the top of the Inspector.

When the Inspector is closed, you obviously have more prime real estate for your programming workspace in the Arrange area. When it's open, this column reveals the heart of information for MIDI quantizing, audio quantizing, and other essential parameters of the active track and all its regions.

There are two parameter boxes above the channel strip that have small black disclosure triangles next to each, allowing you to individually open and collapse those parameter boxes as needed.

Let's start with the one on top, the Region Parameter box. The region name at the top of this box updates depending on what you have selected in the Arrange workspace. It can be confusing. If you highlight the track in the track list but don't have any region selected, it will be labeled MIDI Thru. Once you select a particular region, the parameter box's name will update accordingly.

This is the Region Parameter box, which has the most advanced quantize parameters you'll find on planet Earth. It will be covered in chapter 3, "Writing Your First Track in Logic."

The Track Parameter box is the parameter box shown below, and it shows vital specs for the active track that is highlighted in the track list. These parameters include the track's visual icon (double-click to change), the MIDI channel (if working with a multitimbral MIDI instrument), and parameters related to the track's Flex mode (covered in chapter 9, "Remixing and Making Beats").

Feel free to collapse either of these parameter boxes when you're not using them by clicking on the disclosure triangle in the upper left of each parameter box. If you're working on a smaller laptop screen, you may want to collapse them in order to view the full channel strip, especially if you have a lot of plug-ins loaded.

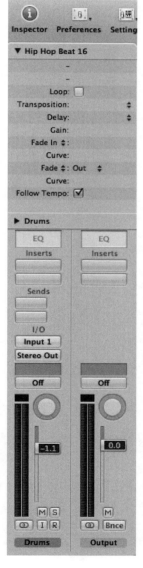

The Inspector

The Region Parameter box   The Track Parameter box

This tour has officially concluded, and you should have all the basic Logic vocabulary you need to get to work. It is time to start writing and discovering the power of Logic's tools for creating music.

Chapter 3
WRITING YOUR FIRST TRACK IN LOGIC

This chapter is for new users and not-so-new users. You will learn more of the essential vocabulary for writing in Logic and tricks to spice up even your first track.

The accompanying DVD-ROM has a QuickTime movie of a Logic project that demonstrates the tools explained in this chapter. The QuickTime movie starts with playback of the finished track, is followed by the parts being deleted, and is then rebuilt step-by-step so you can watch the tools and tricks in action.

Follow along and then write your own first track using the tools demonstrated. This first creation will be "in the box," using Logic's software instruments to get you familiar with the basic layout and the tools in the Arrange window before you get into the variables of signal flow involved with live instruments (which is introduced in chapter 4, "Essential Audio Recording and Mixing in Logic"). For the not-so-new users, this will be a great creative exercise to explore a workflow that's different from your own while you're writing your next track.

Programming Drums

To Do:

- In the Arrange window, choose File > New.
- Select the Empty Project template in view.
- Create three software instrument tracks in the New Tracks dialog box.
- Select Inst 1 in the track list.
- From the Library, select the Drums & Percussion folder.
- Chose the subfolder Electronic Drum Kits.
- Choose Roland TR-808 Kit.

When you launch Logic, the main Arrange window will be in view. From the File menu choose New. Then, in the Templates dialog box that opens, choose the Empty Project template. Select to create three software instrument tracks. The third software instrument track will be highlighted by default and the Settings Library should automatically open on the right to a display of channel strip settings using the software instruments. Navigate from the Drums & Percussion folder to the Electronic Drum Kits, and then select Roland TR-808.

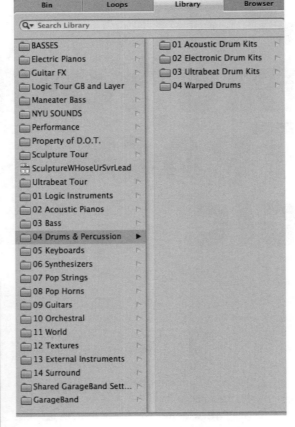

The Drums & Percussion folder in the Settings Library

Channel Strip Settings

When the Roland TR-808 kit is loaded, you will see the software instrument and effects plug-ins populated in the channel strip to the far left of the Arrange window (in this case, the EXS24 sampler loaded with a Logic Compressor and Channel EQ chain). This configuration of an instrument with effects plug-ins is called a *channel strip setting*. This particular channel strip setting has been factory named as "Roland TR-808 Kit". The label is visible on the top pane of the channel strip.

Power Tip: Your Own Channel Strip Settings

How to build your own channel strip settings is one of the most fundamental concepts that you can learn to be a power user and ultimately create your own sound in Logic. See chapter 7, "Creating with Logic's Software Instruments," to learn how.

Plug-in Window View and the Contextual View of Library

Double-clicking and single-clicking on the various panes of the highlighted track's channel strip will speed up your workflow dramatically once you understand how to do it.

The channel strip setting with EXS24, Compressor, and Channel EQ

Double-click on any of the blue panes on the channel strip to open a plug-in window (the instrument insert with the EXS24 or the effects plug-in inserts above where the Logic Compressor and Channel EQ are loaded). For now, go ahead and double-click on the EXS24 on the selected channel strip to see the GUI of this instrument. The EXS24 is the most essential instrument in Logic, even if you choose to supplement it with other third-party samplers and drum instruments. (It will be covered in more detail in chapter 7, "Creating with Logic's Software Instruments.")

Plug-in window view of the EXS24 Interface

Keep in mind that when the Library is visible, single-clicking on any of the blue panes on the channel strip will change the focus of the Library to show all possible settings for an individual plug-in or the channel strip setting itself. In other words, the Library is contextual and updates depending on what is selected on the channel strip of the track highlighted in the track list. The Library view can be a bit confusing if you don't grasp that it is contextual.

Enabling Cycle
In the bar ruler above the Arrange area, you can see that the first four bars are shaded. If you click in the shaded area, you will enable a cycle of those first four bars. Go ahead and do that now, and watch the area turn green. Hit the Spacebar, and the play head (the vertical indicator of your position in the song) will start cycling through the four bars.

Power Tip: Cycling in Logic
Logic refers to repeating an area of a song as *cycling*, though some other music software applications may refer to it as *looping*.

Adjusting Cycle Length
To shorten the cycle region to two bars, hover over the right side of the shaded green cycle selection in the bar ruler and the Pointer will change into a bracket-shaped tool that you can use to adjust the cycle length. Drag it to the left to shorten to two bars.

Adjusting Tempo

In the transport, the tempo defaults to 120 bpm. Double-click on that numeric value to enter a new one. Let's slow it down to 90 bpm.

Adjusting tempo in the transport

Enable the metronome during playback by hitting the button in the transport with the icon of a metronome on the far right. The button will turn blue.

The Metronome in transport

Rehearsing Your Drum Parts

Hit the Spacebar to start playback so that you can rehearse an exchange of kick and snare. Keep it simple.

Recording the Kick and Snare with the Click

The Record button is on the left side of the transport near the other basic transport controls of Play, Pause, and so on. If you hover over the transport controls, an information bar pops up letting you know which is the Record button. When you're ready, hit Record.

The metronome will provide a one-bar count-off so that you can start right on bar 1, beat 1. The count-off can be adjusted in the Recording Settings (Settings > Recording), covered in the section called "Record Settings: Count-In and Click" in chapter 4, "Essential Audio Recording and Mixing in Logic."

After the one-bar count-off in Record mode, play a simple kick-and-snare pattern for two bars, and then stop.

The Record button in transport

Understanding Regions

A *region* is the fundamental building block of all your writing. The region object in the Arrange workspace on a track can contain audio or MIDI data. There are many editing parameters that can be applied to a region from the upper left parameter box, most notably quantization to adjust the timing and swing.

Looping the Recording

Hit the "L" on your keyboard, and the two-bar region you played will loop indefinitely. You have just used your first Logic key command! The shortcuts in Logic are covered in chapter 6, "The Secret to Learning Logic: Key Commands." If you don't want the two bars to keep repeating, disable the Cycle button in the transport on the right (with the two curved arrows that are pointing to each other in a circle).

The Cycle button in transport

We could make a specific number of copies using a different key command (the Repeat Regions key command). But while I'm in the writing mode, I don't like to worry about how many times I need a particular region to repeat, I just want it to keep playing. Using the Loop Regions key command, the region will not have true copies but rather *aliases*, which are explained next.

Loop regions using the default key command "L"

Power Tip: Real Copies Versus Aliases

Real copies of a region are independent regions that can be edited and modified independently in the Region Parameter box. Aliases are quick copies of a region that will follow all the behavior of the original region as far as any assignments in the Region Parameter box for example, Quantize, Delay, Dynamics, and so on).

Quantizing Basics

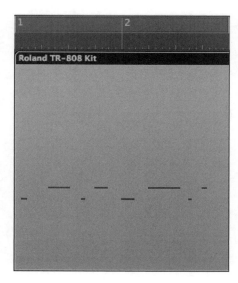

Logic can quantize all the data in a region or quantize individual events in the Piano Roll editor and other events editors. Here we will look at quantizing by region. Highlight the two-bar region so that the region header turns black. The region header is the area at the top of the region where the name is visible.

The Region Parameter Box

Now you can quantize your work. The Region Parameter box in the upper left is active for whatever region you have selected in the main workspace. You can have two regions next to each other in the Arrange area with different quantizing values (for example, one straight, the next swinging, one on eighth notes, while the next region is on 16th notes. Using different quantize settings from one region to the next can give your project a more human feel if used musically, as though the band were tastefully building the groove. Go ahead and experiment with the quantize value and feel for your Kick and Snare exchange.

Selected region and the region header

The Region Parameter box

Region Quantize

Let's quantize to eighth notes by clicking-and-holding to the right of Quantize in the Region Parameter box, either on the Up/Down Arrow keys or on top of where the word defaults to "off (3840)".

Either way, a pull-down menu will be revealed where you can select your quantize value. Scroll up to the choice of 1/8-note, then release. The quantizing tools in Logic's Region Parameter box are phenomenal for adjusting every nuance of your swing and groove feel (this is covered in greater detail in chapter 9, "Remixing and Making Beats."

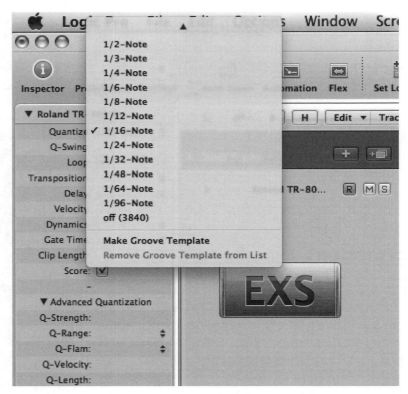

Region quantize

Create New Track with Same Settings

Above track 1 are two plus signs for different types of New Track creation. The one on the left will open up the same Create Track dialog box that launches automatically when you open an Empty Project template. Click on the one on the right, and you will create a new track that has the same channel strip setting as does the track that is highlighted when you select it. Do that now so you create a new track with the TR-808 Kit.

Adjusting Your Region Length

Let's program hi-hats using this second TR-808 Kit with a simple, steady eighth-note pattern for two bars. If you accidentally play beyond the two bars, drag the lower right corner of the region to the left to shorten it. The playhead turns into a bracket-shaped tool when you find the spot on the region that allows you to adjust the region length.

Go ahead and quantize your hi-hats by highlighting the region, and then selecting the quantize value in the Region Parameter box to the left.

Copying a Region

Now let's make a copy of the hi-hats region by highlighting and then Option-dragging the region to the right. The copied hi-hat region should appear in bars 3 and 4.

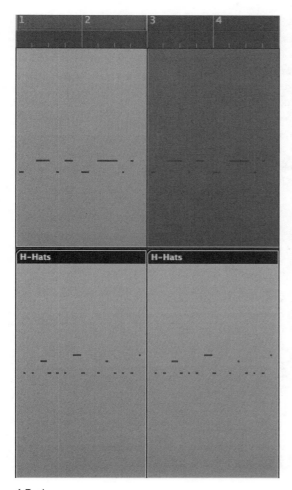

A Region copy

Selecting the Right Sound for Your Synth Part

Before you start recording, give yourself time to shop for the sound. Having the right character sound can inspire the right part, and Logic's palette of channel strip settings in the Library is a great place to start exploring.

To Do:

- Select Instrument 2 in the track list.
- Load an electric piano (Library > Keyboards > Electric Pianos > Stage Piano Mk 1).
- Hit the Spacebar to play back the recorded drums, then experiment until you find a two-chord progression.
- Feel free to select a new channel strip setting in the Library after recording your part.

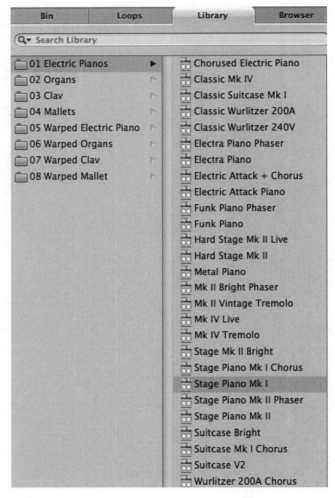

Library submenus of electric pianos

Recording While Viewing Notation

- Select the tab labeled Score, below the Arrange area.
- Hit Record and play your two-bar chord progression.

You will be able to watch the notation right while you are recording! You can also hit this Editor tab after a MIDI track is recorded to view the recorded notation. Keep in mind that you can edit notes in the Score Editor as well.

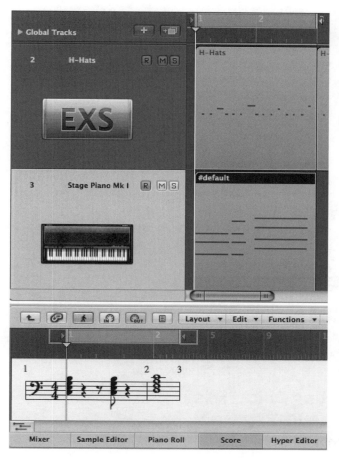

The Score Editor

Saving Your Project the Right Way

Stop! Do not go any further without saving your Logic project. Ideally, this step should be taken after the first note is recorded (if not prior to recording the first note).

In the File menu, select Save As.... The Save As dialog box will pop open so that you can name the project and direct its path on your hard drive.

If you haven't already, create a folder on your drive for all the Logic projects that will you be creating. Then in the Save As dialog box, place the current Logic project in that path. You can create a Songs folder inside this Save As dialog box, with the New Folder button at the bottom left of the window.

Power Tip: Include Project Assets

This is one of the most important habits you can develop early on while doing your production work in Logic. Make sure that all the Asset checkboxes are checked in the Include Assets dialog box. The only exception might be the Copy Movie Files To Project Folder checkbox, if you aren't working with QuickTime Movies in the project.

This will be discussed further in chapter 11, "Good Housekeeping and Other Smart Practices."

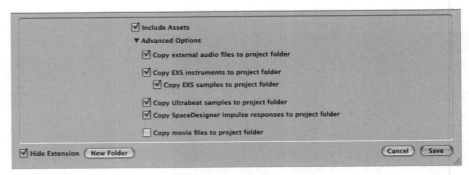

Include assets when saving a Logic project

Once you set the file path, any audio or settings you introduce to the project will automatically save into this project folder. There's never a reason not to have your EXS samples, audio files, or any other Logic assets saved with your Logic song.

A Few Tricks to Help Your Creative Process

The following tricks are not really "tricks" but popular MIDI features that have been in Logic for years. They have helped establish Logic's reputation as the tool of choice for the musician creating complete arrangements of music projects.

Quick Trick #1: Creating Quick "Fills" (Time-Compressing MIDI)

- Select the instrument track with the hi-hats you programmed; highlight the copied region in bars 3 through 4.
- Hold down the Option key, and then hover in the lower right corner of region in bar 4 until the playhead turns into a bracket-shaped tool.
- Drag to the left, halfway through the region, the length of one bar, and then release. Make sure that you hold the Option key throughout the operation.
- Move this time-compressed region over to the right so that it lies on bar 4.
- The original hi-hat region should alias a copy to fill bar 3. If it doesn't, select the first region and hit the "L" key.
- Shut the metronome in the transport and hit the Spacebar to play back.

You have just used one of the oldest tricks in the Logic book for time-compressing MIDI—in this case, to make it sound like the drummer "got busy" at bar 4.

Quick Trick #2: Separating the Drums— an Arranging Tool

- Highlight track 1 with the Kick and Snare.
- Select the local menu for MIDI. Local menus are the smaller row of menu items specific to an editor, whether in the Arrange or Mixer window. In the Arrange window, they are located directly above the bar ruler.
- From the pull-down menu, select Separate MIDI Events.

- From the submenu to the right, select By Note Pitch.
- The Kick and Snare are now isolated from each other on separate tracks. They are actually independent regions, although both are being triggered from the same EXS24 instrument.
- You can now adjust the Kick to begin at a different start time than the Snare, because they are independent regions. Select the Kick region and hit the Loop Regions key command that defaults to "L".
- Slide the Snare region over to bar 3 so that it makes an entrance two bars after the Kick.

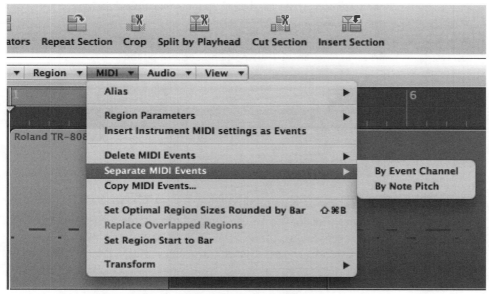

Local MIDI menu to separate drums by note pitch

Keep in mind that the Kick and Snare are still coming out of the same software instrument, the same instance of the EXS24. You can't use the volume slider on the channel strip to adjust relative volumes, but you can adjust the individual velocities of each region in the Region Parameter box or the Piano Roll editor. For quick arrangement purposes like the above, this isolation can be extremely helpful.

Quick Trick #3: Capture As Recording (Never Lose a Performance!)

This feature is one of Logic's coolest tools for the creative writing process. It's human nature that we often come up with our greatest ideas when we're just messing around in the studio, playing, jamming, and riffing on a track with no intention of recording a take. With Capture As Recording, these MIDI performances are never lost. For many of us, it can be an unconscious reflex to tense up when the Record button is enabled and the bar ruler turns bright red, even when you're working alone in the studio. With Capture As Recording, there is no need to hit the Record button—you wait until after you create a MIDI performance you like. Logic holds your MIDI performance in a buffer for as long as the track is in play mode. You can use the Capture As Recording key command or the Transport button either while the track is still in play mode or when it has stopped before you begin playback again.

- With the first Electric Piano chord track highlighted, select the Create Track button on the right at the top of the track list. This will create a new track using the same plug-in settings. Note: Be sure to highlight the track in the track list and not the region in the Arrange workspace.
- With a new Electric Piano track selected, enable playback in Logic with the Spacebar and start noodling around.
- When you find a riff with a nice feel, stop playback by hitting the Spacebar. Don't worry about trying to re-create your performance.
- Select the Capture Recording button (which looks like a bull's eye) to the right of the Record button in the transport. The MIDI data for what you just played will appear onscreen. Logic has captured your performance!
- Note: If the Capture Recording button is not in view, Control-click in the empty space of the Transport bar area to Customize Transport and add this button.

Capture Recording button

Power Tip: Capture As Recording in Real Time

The Capture As Recording feature can be used in real time while the transport is still running for as long as it remains running, or once playback has stopped before you resume playback. You can still assign this as a key command if you find that to be quicker. Or just tap this transport button after adding it with the Customize Transport dialog box.

Hopefully your little track idea is a keeper!

Chapter 4

ESSENTIAL AUDIO RECORDING AND MIXING IN LOGIC

This chapter will cover the basics of recording audio and mixing in Logic. If you're approaching these tasks from the vantage point of a creative musician who has to deliver a high-quality mix by yourself, without the assistance of a professional engineer, have no fear. You will find the tools you need to achieve great results recording and mixing inside Logic in this chapter. You will be introduced to features unique to Logic that help the mixing process with or without an engineering background.

This chapter assumes that you have set up and tested your sound input and output whether you are using a built-in or an external audio interface. It is also a premise that you've made the proper input and output assignments in your Audio Preferences, as covered in chapter 1's section, "Connecting External Hardware." If not, please do so now.

You can use the basic Logic project created in the previous chapter to now record vocals, guitar, or any live instrument in your studio. Or start a new project from the Empty Project template and simply talk into the microphone, whether an external mic or the built-in mic. If you're not feeling any lyrical inspiration, pick any passage from this chapter to read out loud.

Recording Audio

Setting up to record audio in Logic is surprisingly fast, beginning with the implementation of the New Track button for configuring your new record tracks. Beyond that, the automatic creation of the Logic project folder from the Save As dialog box will ensure that all your audio files are stored conveniently for retrieval and backup.

Create an Audio Track

Create new audio tracks in the Arrange window with the New Track button at the top of the track list.

Create Tracks button.

The New Track button opens the same dialog box that pops up when launching Logic from the Empty Project template. Here, you select how many tracks you need, which type (audio, software instrument, and so on), and the input and output assignment, which can be modified later directly on the channel strip in the Arrange window and the Mixer view.

Mono Versus Stereo

In the New Tracks dialog box, you can choose mono or stereo inputs and outputs when the track type is Audio. Inputs and outputs are naturally selected independently.

First, use the Format pull-down menu to toggle between Mono Input and Stereo Input.

Under Input, choose which input number(s) of your audio interface you'd like to use. The number of inputs available depends on your audio interface and not on Logic.

Under the Output assignment are the available outputs. The number displayed depends on your audio interface (whether it has 2, 4, 8, or 16 channels or more). If you are using Built-In sound, you will see only Stereo Output available. All other outputs will be grayed out.

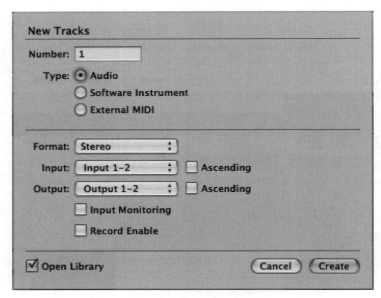

New Tracks dialog box for Mono/Stereo and Input/Output assignment

Go ahead and create one mono audio track, then highlight it in the track list of the Arrange window.

Arming a Track to Record

Be sure that the Record Enable button (labeled "R") is checked so the track is armed. That means recording is enabled on the track and will begin as soon as you select Record in the transport or by key command. Arming the track is distinct from highlighting or selecting the track. The track must be armed via this button on the designated track(s) in the track list, on its channel strip in the Arrange window or in the Mixer.

The Record Arm button on the track header

Setting Record Levels

Once you record-arm the track, you are ready to check levels and begin recording. You should immediately see the signal indicator jumping on the fader as well as on the track header to the left of its name in the track list.

Just as with any professional analog tape recorder, you do not set the input recording levels in Logic, or in any DAW for that matter. The fader on the channel strip in Logic for the corresponding record track indicates the monitor level only. You need to make any necessary adjustments in your signal path before it reaches Logic. Record levels must be set on either your mixer, your mic pre, or your audio interface—wherever signal is being fed into Logic.

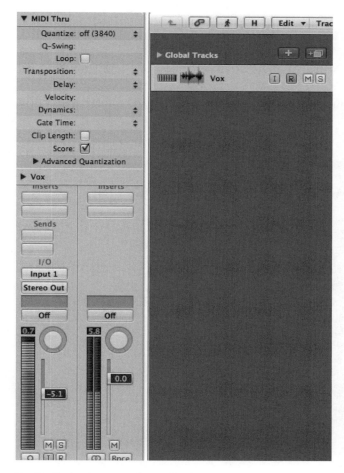

The Monitor level on a record-armed track

Power Tip: Pre-Fader Metering

A very helpful feature for checking input level is the Pre-Fader Metering option in the Arrange window (Options >Audio > Pre-Fader Metering).

Setting the Record Path to Your Logic Project

A Logic song is defined as a Logic project. The audio files are set to record to an audio file folder within the project folder as long as you enable the checkbox "Copy external audio files to project folder". This simplifies your file management and occurs automatically when you select Save As from the File menu and name your project.

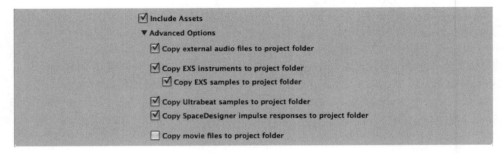

Setting the record path

Record Settings: Count-In and Click

The quick way to adjust the Count-In is to click-and-hold on the Record switch in the transport and open the Recording Settings. Here you can adjust how many bars the count-in will be.

You can also access this menu (Settings > Recording) from the toolbar on top of the Arrange window.

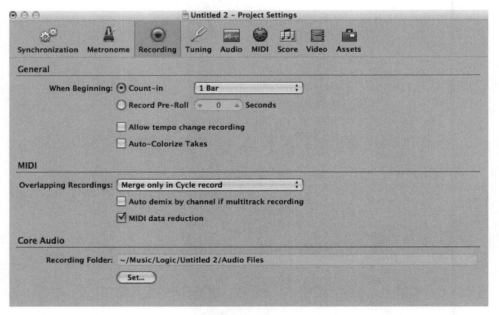

Record Settings for count-in

The click should default to being enabled when you start recording. If not, launch the Record Settings, select the Metronome icon to the left of Recording, and then enable the click at the bottom of the Options menu.

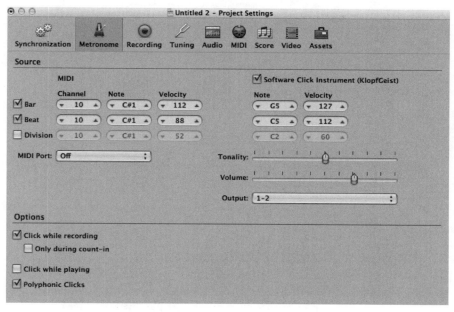

Metronome Settings for the click

Power Tip: Eighth-Note Metronome Click for Drummers

Sometimes musicians, especially drummers, will request a click track with a smaller denominator of clicks than quarter-note beats, especially with slow ballads. To enable eighth or even 16th-note clicks, first enable Division in the Metronome Settings by either choosing Settings in the toolbar or clicking-and-holding on the Click icon in the transport. Then set the Division value, directly under the Time Signature in the transport, accordingly.

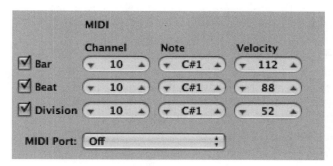

Metronome click on eighth notes

Sample Rate in the Audio Settings

The Sample Rate assignment is also made in the Audio Settings. Logic can support up to a 192 kHz sample rate, depending what your audio interface is capable of. Keep in mind that any audio you import will automatically conform to Logic's current sample rate.

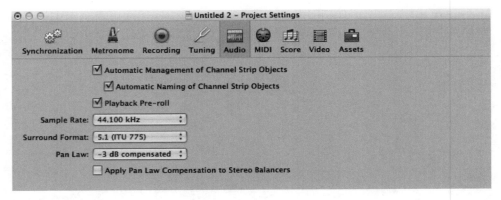

Assigning sample rate

This is different from the sample rate that you bounce at (which is defined in the Bounce menu).

Power Tip: Settings Versus Preferences

The difference between Settings and Preferences may seem like an arbitrary distinction in Logic, but it's actually a powerful one. When preparing to record, you may need to navigate to your Audio Preferences as well as your Settings for Record, Metronome, and Audio to make adjustments. It's easy to get dyslexic about where to find a feature. Here's the golden rule: Preferences are global and Settings are generally assigned per Logic project. For example, if you adjust the count-in or the sample rate in a particular project, the next time you start a project from the Empty Project template, the Count-In will default to one bar and the Sample Rate to 44.1 kHz.

Naming a Record Track

Read this section carefully! Most Logic users are extremely sloppy when it comes to naming their tracks and respective audio files. Tracks are named in the track list by double-clicking on the default title (for example, Audio 1, Audio 2, and so on). It's best to name the track before you start recording. That way all the created audio regions will conform to the correct name and it will be easier to search for these files in the Bin to the right of the Arrange window. A common and dangerous mistake is to skip over naming the audio track in advance, and then ending up with tons of recorded audio files that are generically named, for example, "Audio 2." You can always go into the Audio Bin to rename audio files if you are careless when recording.

Power Tip: Name Your Tracks Before You Record

Name your tracks before you start recording in order to avoid the chaos of not being able to easily search for a particular recording. Think of it like creating a track sheet in the days of tape. If you realize after you record that you want to rename the track, remember that the audio files in the Bin did not update! The track may now be labeled "Lead Vocal" in the track list and in the Mixer, while the audio in the Bin is still called "Audio 2". If you do rename the track, be smart and go into the Bin and rename the associated audio file by double-clicking on the file name, which will have a disclosure triangle to the left. When the disclosure triangle is opened, it reveals all the regions of the audio file that will subsequently get renamed if you do rename the audio file.

Multi-Take Recording Basics

A longtime request from Logic users was to incorporate playlists, as commonly used in Pro Tools. The implementation of Multi-Take Recording in Logic has a great advantage in that all the takes can be viewed simultaneously.

There is no setup involved with Multi-Take Recording. You simply record again on the same track and a take folder is automatically created. The visual indications that a track has multiple performances recorded are the sideways-pointed triangle in the upper left of the region header and the downward pointing triangle in the upper right of the region header.

The take folder

Clicking on the triangle in the upper left will reveal all of your individual takes. To audition, simply highlight the desired take region with your Pointer tool and begin playback.

Previewing the take folder

Punch-In Recording: Record Toggle

A common recording practice is to "punch in," meaning you record into a previously recorded passage. Punching in allows you to seamlessly fix a mistake on an otherwise great recording, and have it seem as though it was all done at once.

To engage recording while in playback mode is referred to as recording "on the fly." To punch-in record, start playback, and manually press Shift + R, the default key command for Record Toggle, at the point where you want to start recording. Audio recording will start immediately. Hit the Record Toggle key again, and the sequencer will continue to play but recording will stop.

One setting must be enabled. Click-and-hold the record button in the transport and the Record menu will open, allowing you to switch on Punch On The Fly.

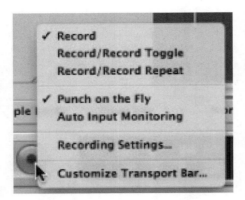

Punch On The Fly

Autopunch Recording

This practice allows you to define the area to punch in advance. Enable the Autopunch button in the transport. A shaded red area appears in the bar ruler—thinner than the Cycle area—that you can adjust to define where recording will be replaced.

Autopunch

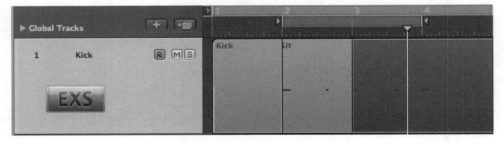

Autopunch indication in lower half of bar ruler

Sneak preview! In chapter 5, "Navigating and Editing Made Simple," under the heading "The Marquee Tool: Your Secret Weapon in Logic," you'll find another trick for Autopunch recording.

Mixing Your Music

The Logic Mixer has come into its own as being both professional and technically sound. While historically the mixer has not been Logic's strongpoint, in recent years it has incorporated features that are greatly appreciated by longtime Logic users and increasingly by professional engineers.

The Mixer is accessed from the main Arrange window from the tab at the bottom of the screen labeled, appropriately, Mixer. This is a toggle to bring the Mixer into and out of view. Whichever track is highlighted in the Arrange window will be selected in the Mixer, indicated with a lime-green rectangle around the channel strip.

The Mixer tab and a selected track in Mixer

Track input and output assignments can be easily modified on the channel strip, beneath the Sends and Inserts, where it is labeled I/O for Input and Output assignment.

Channel Strip Settings for Mixing

Creating channel strip settings is an example of a Logic mixing feature that has sped up the workflow for every Logic user who has discovered it. While channel strip settings are immediately visible in the main Arrange window and part of the Arrange window

I/O assignment on the channel strip

workflow, they are also an essential part of the work done in the Logic Mixer. Even Pro Tools engineers have their eyes on this innovative system for saving and reloading an entire plug-in chain. Channel strip settings are a configuration of plug-ins that combine, for example, a nice EQ setting and a compressor setting that work well together for a specific purpose. At the top of each channel strip is the pane for the channel strip setting.

There are tons of fantastic factory channel strip settings that contain a combination of plug-ins and their settings for specific mixing purposes, whether for problem solving or for creating a particular sound like a Clean Acoustic Guitar or a Warm Acoustic Guitar. They are grouped into categories by an instrument (Drums & Percussion, Electric Guitar, and so on) or by Voice.

There are also highly creative channel strip settings in the folders labeled Spaces, Warped, and Surround. The channel strip settings are available for not only audio tracks and software instrument tracks, but also for the Main Output track—in effect, mastering and analysis settings. I have seen the Logic sessions of more than a few "hit" songs that have used Logic channel strip settings straight from the factory.

Where it really gets powerful is when you start modifying the factory channel strip settings or creating your own from scratch for specific purposes, such as for your guitarist or your singer. These combinations of EQs, Compressors, Reverbs, and many more of Logic's 80-plus effects plug-ins can be used right from the start, so that as soon as the artist gets on the mic, he or she immediately sounds good. After you tweak a plug-in chain for a particular situation or song, my recommendation is to save it as a channel strip setting, maybe with a keyword from the song name, so it shows up in your Library the next time your guitarist or singer is in the same mood, working on, for example, another ballad or an up-tempo dance track.

The great news is that third-party plug-ins can be stored in the chain of a channel strip setting as well.

Channel Strip Settings

Power Tip: Using Software Instrument Settings on Audio Tracks

You may find yourself working on the plug-in chain for a bass line recorded by a live bass player, then remember a perfect plug-in chain you created for the ES1 software instrument. The channel strip settings for software instruments and audio tracks are technically saved to separate folders, such as Track, Master, Instrument, and so on. You can see this organization when you look from the Finder. But Logic has a great solution for this fairly common dilemma. Option-click on the Channel Strip Setting pane on top of a channel strip to access Channel Strip Settings from a different type of track object—for example, a software instrument channel strip setting even though you're working on an audio track.

Option-click to access all channel strip setting types

Creating Your Own Channel Strip Settings

Create your own channel strip settings that will then be available within the Library to the right of the Arrange window. To create your own channel strip setting, click-and-hold on the pane labeled Setting, at the top of the channel strip setting. A menu appears with the Save Channel Strip Setting option. You can also scroll through the Library of existing channel strip settings from this pull-down menu, but I recommend developing the habit of shopping for channel strip settings in the Library on the right side of the Arrange window.

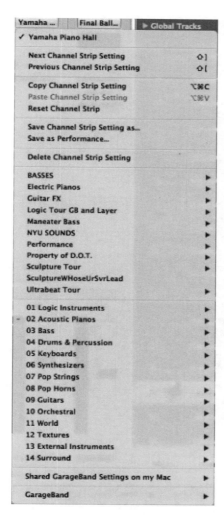

The Channel Strip Setting menu

Channel strip settings will be discussed further in chapter 7, "Creating with Logic's Software Instruments." The more time and attention you give to designing channel strip settings in Logic, the more you will create your own sound in Logic and truly make it your instrument.

Single Mode Versus Arrange Mode

The mode buttons in the Mixer are an incredibly functional system that will speed up your workflow enormously. They are located in the upper right of the screen and are labeled Single, Arrange, and All. Whichever mode button is selected determines which group of tracks are in view.

Mixer mode buttons

Arrange mode is the most straightforward, displaying all the tracks in the Arrange window of the current project. Single mode is brilliant and unique to the Logic Mixer. This gives you a view of the entire signal flow of a selected track, whether an audio track or a software instrument. The main channel strip (of the track highlighted in the Arrange track list) will be visible along with any auxiliary tracks and the main output, so you can isolate and focus on the complete sound and signal path.

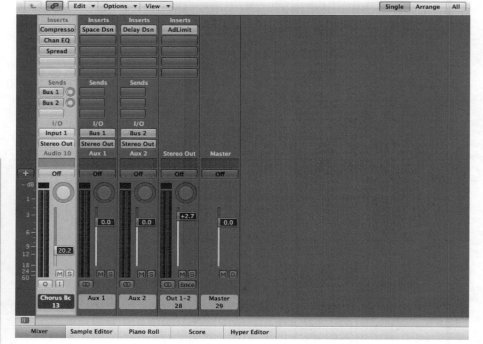

Single mode in the Mixer

Bussing to an aux on dual channel strips in the Arrange window

This eliminates the traditionally laborious process of scrolling in your mixer past all the 32, 64, or more audio tracks to the auxiliary tracks where a vocal is bussed, for example. Between the two features of Single mode and dynamic channel strip creation in the Arrange window (the Dual Channel strip), you can easily follow the workflow practices of the professional engineer as far as bussing plug-ins to auxiliary tracks. The secondary (and in some cases more significant) benefit is maximizing an efficient CPU load on your computer. For example, instead of creating the same plug-in chain on each of the four background vocals with an EQ, Compressor, and Reverb using the same exact setting, you can create busses to one auxiliary track with all three plug-ins or three individual auxiliary tracks. Either way, you will only have each effect loaded one time: 3 instead of 12 plug-ins bogging down your CPU.

"All" mode in the Mixer is simply all possible tracks: audio tracks, software instrument tracks, auxiliary tracks, and so on. There are many instances in which this becomes useful: if, for example, you need to view and adjust the level of the Klopgeist, Logic's peculiarly named metronome, which defaults to the last available software instrument (Inst 256) and is not in the Arrange window view by default.

The other set of Mixer mode buttons to be aware of are the buttons to the right that are labeled Audio, Inst, Aux, Bus, Input, Output, Master, and MIDI. These will isolate a type of track within each mode view you select—Single, Arrange, or All. This is handy when you want to temporarily focus on your software instruments or aux tracks, for example.

The mode buttons are helpful when you are revisiting an older project you haven't looked at in a while, getting familiar with someone else's Logic project, or simply working quickly in your own session.

Mixer Trick #1: Rearranging and Bypassing FX

The Mixer has a tool menu independent of the one in the Arrange window, as do all the Editor windows. The Hand tool is a great choice for the secondary tool in the Mixer: holding down the Command/Apple key accesses the Hand tool, allowing you to rearrange plug-ins on a track or between tracks. Simply highlight and drag up or down in the plug-in chain with the Hand tool. Additionally hold down the Option key while selecting the Hand tool to copy a plug-in to another track.

Hand tool to rearrange plug-ins

To bypass a plug-in, Option-click and the plug-in will remain on the channel strip but appear grayed out. You may want to bypass a plug-in for A/B'ing purposes, or it may be a creative decision to automate the bypass during a particular passage.

Option-click to bypass a plug-in

Mixer Trick #2: Coloring Track Names

The track names at the bottom of each channel strip can be color coded just like your markers and regions in the Arrange window. It takes only a few extra seconds to do this and you'll thank yourself. It looks and feels great, like when you shine your shoes! Practically speaking, your eye can quickly adjust to the visual grouping, and this becomes a subtle workflow enhancement in that you are able to find a particular instrument more quickly. For example, all your vocals can have a background color of red, all your drums can be blue, and so on. To change the color, select Colors from the local View menu at the bottom of the list, and then swipe across the track names at the bottom of the channel strips. Or, you can use the default key command, Option + C.

Coloring your Mixer track names

Mixer Trick #3: Temporary Track Grouping

Creating groups in Logic will be covered in chapter 5, "Navigating and Editing Made Simple." While we're here in the Mixer, there is a great way to temporarily group tracks for adjusting gain, adding a Send, and so on. Drag over adjacent tracks, and they will become highlighted and placed in a temporary group. To add nonadjacent tracks, hold down the Shift key as you drag over the tracks.

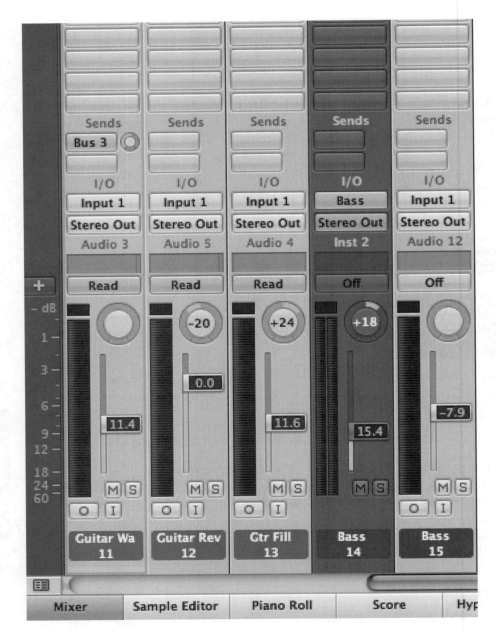

Temporary track grouping in the Mixer

Chapter 5
NAVIGATING AND EDITING MADE SIMPLE

This chapter may be the most important one in the whole book. Your Logic workflow will take flight if you begin to master even part of the potential and flexibility of Logic's tools. This is, of course, no guarantee that your music will sound better, but these tools are as fundamental and satisfying to the writing experience as the right cooking utensils in the kitchen are for cooking.

In particular, we will cover the Marquee tool in depth. If you strive to work with speed and precision in Logic, the Marquee tool should be second only to the Pointer.

Know Your Navigation Tools

Logic's navigation tools are second nature to any serious Logic user, yet possibly the first thing to trip up a new Logic user, especially one more familiar with Pro Tools. The Logic design for tool switching is intuitive and fast if you give yourself a chance to wrap your head around the following: the Tool menus, the Escape key shortcut for switching tools with the floating toolbox and, for many Logic users, the Pointer tool Click Zones.

The Pointer Tool and Tool Menus

The Pointer tool and Tool menus were introduced in chapter 2's tour of the Arrange window. The Tool menus are located in the upper right of the Arrange window. There are also independent Tool menus in the same location of every editor—in the Mixer, Sample Editor, Piano Roll, Score, and even Hyper Editor. You can always grab any tool from the primary menu on the left, or assign any tool to the Command-click tool menu on the right. To access the alternate tool, hold down the Command/Apple key.

The Escape key was the original way to access tools in Logic and is still very slick and convenient. When you hit the Escape key, a floating toolbox appears wherever your Pointer tool is. The floating toolbox allows you to select another tool without having to move your eye from its current focal point and lose concentration. The toolbox comes to you.

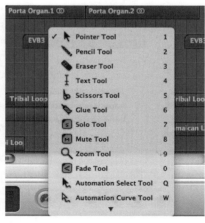

The floating toolbox via the Escape key

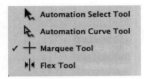

The Marquee tool

The Marquee Tool: Your Secret Weapon in Logic

Quite simply, the Marquee tool is perhaps the most powerful editing tool in Logic, and it also provides some cool behaviors for navigation. The symbol for it is a plus sign (+).

For Pro Tools users, the Marquee tool is most closely related to the Selector tool. Therefore, with the Pointer tool as the main tool in Logic and the Marquee as the alternate tool, you are most closely replicating the Pro Tools Smart tool (the Hand, Trim, and Selector tools).

Using the Marquee tool, drag across a region or multiple regions across tracks to select. Then, you can quickly perform various edit functions (such as creating dropouts) by muting or deleting parts of a region. You can always extend the start and end point of your Marquee selection with the Shift key. What's fantastic is how easy it is to apply Marquee tool edits in real time, while the transport is running and you're listening back to your project. Especially if there are other musicians in the room, you don't need to interrupt the groove to perform an edit.

Spend some time experimenting with the following powerful Marquee tool navigation and edit functions:

- Marquee Cut: Marquee-select across an area of a region or of multiple regions, and then click into the Marquee-selected area with the Pointer tool by releasing the Command key (if Marquee is your Alternate tool). The area will be snipped on either side, creating an independent region. Or, double-click with your Marquee to make an incision into a region. This will cut the region into two regions.

Marquee-select

With Marquee Cut, there is no longer any reason to use the older Scissors tool for basic cutting. The Scissors tool requires two separate incisions on either side of an area in order to isolate it into a new region. There is, however, one great Scissors tool trick in chapter 9, "Remixing and Making Beats."

- Marquee Mute: Marquee-select across an area of a region or of multiple regions, and then hit the "M" key to mute the selection. Both sides of the highlighted area will be cut, creating an independent region (or independent regions if you are swiping across tracks).

- Marquee-Option-Copy: Marquee-select across an area of a region or of multiple regions, and then Option-drag to copy the highlighted area to another place in the timeline on the same track or onto another track. The cut from the Marquee selection will be automatically "healed" and no longer visible.

- Marquee-Selection Paste: The Marquee selection can be an insertion point for pasting content from the clipboard. When you click-and-hold with the Marquee tool, a help tag appears indicating what the bars/beats of your location are, so you can make an exact selection in time to place the region or note events.

- Single Pixel Marquee: If you don't know this one, read this section carefully! Click into the Arrange workspace with the Marquee tool to create a thin white vertical line. When you hit the Spacebar to enable playback, the playhead will jump to the Single Pixel Marquee insertion point. Even if there is a Cycle area selected in the bar ruler, the Single Pixel point will take priority as to where playback will start.

  To remove the Single Pixel mark, click anywhere in the workspace with the Pointer.

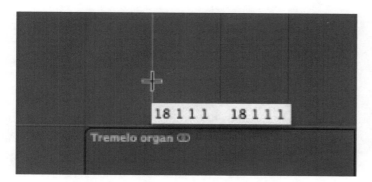

Single Pixel Marquee

- Single Pixel Marquee and Delete Key to Cut: Click into a region in the Arrange workspace with the Marquee tool to create a thin white vertical line. Then, select the Delete key on your keyboard. A cut will be made in the region.
- Marquee Multiple Track Swipe: Swipe across multiple tracks with the Marquee tool to create a region selection across all the tracks. Then use any of the above tools, such as clicking into the highlighted area with the Pointer tool by releasing the Command Key (if Marquee is your alternate tool). Or select mute with the key command "M". This is a great trick for creating a breakdown for one beat, two beats, or a whole bar.

Marquee select across tracks

- Marquee-Select Empty Space: This is a big one. When you cut, copy, or paste a Marquee selection, the empty space in the selection is included. This is perfect for editing regions that don't start on the downbeat of a bar or even right on a beat. After making the selection, you must apply the keystrokes Command + C to copy, then Command + V to paste at the new location. Unfortunately, Option-drag does not work in this situation for copying the selected area.

Marquee-select empty space

- Set Locators by Marquee: Set a cycle area by your Marquee selection simply by clicking on the Set Locators tool in the toolbar after making a Marquee selection. This Set Locators tool works for regions as well. Once selected, you can easily repeat, insert, and cut within the locators.

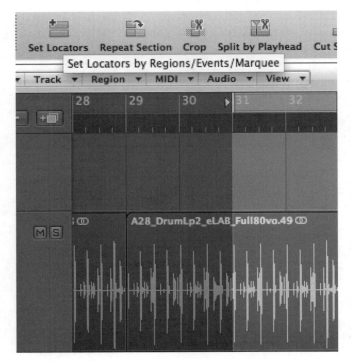

Set Locators by Marquee

- Marquee Snap to Transients (Tab to Transient): Tab to transient is the Pro Tools term for using the Tab key to jump forward and backward between transients. Transients are the peaks in your audio when you are completely zoomed in. Logic implemented a similar feature with the Marquee tool.

Click into the audio file with the Marquee tool, then use your Left and Right Arrow keys to jump to the previous and next transient, respectively (default key commands are called Forward By Transient and Rewind By Transient). It's helpful to be zoomed in enough to really view the transients. If there is a Marquee tool selection, the Right and Left Arrows adjust the end of the selection, snapping to transients. Shift + Left Arrow/ Right Arrow behaves similarly for the left selection border.

- Marquee Cut on Transient: A quick editing technique is to hit the delete key after selecting a transient to make a cut on that transient. Another power trick is to Shift-select between two transients with the Marquee tool so that the area between is shaded. Then, use the delete key to quickly slice on both sides and create a region.

- Quick Swipe Marquee Record: If you have audio on a track and want to record over a section, Marquee-select the part you want to punch-in, and then hit record. The Autopunch light will come on in the transport. It drops into Record mode but records only over the part selected with the Marquee tool. This achieves the same results as enabling Autopunch in the transport then adjusting the thin cycle area in the bar ruler.

- Marquee-Select Automation: Automation has not been covered yet, but it is an essential Marquee tool trick. Marquee-select any area of automation, and four nodes are created to easily draw in volume rides.

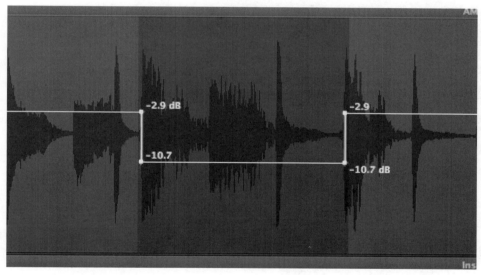

Marquee-Select Automation

Your Zoom Tools

You should learn how to quickly magnify and shrink the scale of viewing regions (or *zoom*) in the Arrange window, using both with key commands and other tools in Logic. Whether you want to enlarge your field of vision and see further along in the timeline, or zoom in tight on a single region, perhaps down to the transient, is a completely dynamic decision. The following tools should be employed often while you work if you intend to work efficiently. Memorize these!

- Ctrl + Option + rubber-band selection

  This is the preferred zoom method for many longtime Logic users and myself. It is fairly unique to Logic and may seem awkward until you get the hang of it. Hold down the Ctrl and Option modifier keys while you drag across the area you want to enlarge in the Arrange window. The Pointer turns into a magnifier glass, representing the Zoom tool. This lasso or rubber-banding with the two modifier keys is an ancient Logic zoom technique that you will become adept at the more you use it. You will start to have a feel for exactly how big an area to select to achieve the right zoom scale. Click into the empty space while still holding the two modifier keys (Ctrl + Option), and the zoom scale reverts to the previous zoom level.

What's nice about this technique is that you are not limited to specific zoom levels (unlike with other DAWs) but can control exactly the desired scale.

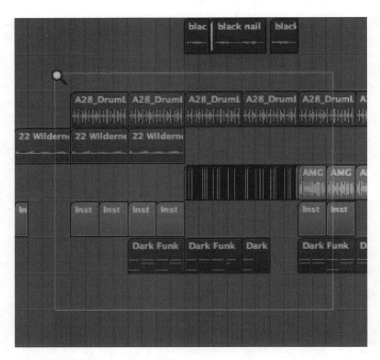

Ctrl + Option + rubber-band selection

- Drag Down from bar ruler with Playhead
  This is a newer zoom technique that some users may prefer. Simply drag down from the bar ruler into the Arrange area with your playhead to zoom in (drag up to zoom out).

Key Commands to Zoom
- Zoom to Fit Selection or All Content: Highlight an area, and then hit Z, assigned to the Z key (for "zoom").
- Zoom to Fit All Contents: Everything in the Arrange window will be fit into view. Recommended assignment is Shift + Z.
- Zoom Horizontal In and Out: Ctrl + Option + Left and Right Arrows, respectively.
- Zoom Vertical In and Out: Ctrl + Option + Up and Down Arrows, respectively.

Caps Lock Keyboard: No Controller Necessary
This feature represents the ultimate freedom in Logic. You truly need only your computer to write music in Logic and no external hardware to input MIDI events. Click on the Caps Lock key, and your computer keyboard becomes a controller for inputting MIDI notes into Logic. A light gray-scale graphic representation of the keyboard appears onscreen, providing visual feedback of which musical note you're triggering from the QWERTY keyboard. The number keys on top switch octaves, and the bottom

row of the keyboard (Z, X, C, V…) allow you to adjust velocity. The Caps Lock key is a toggle, so you simply click a second time to disable the feature. With a little practice you can input drum tracks and bass lines, even chords.

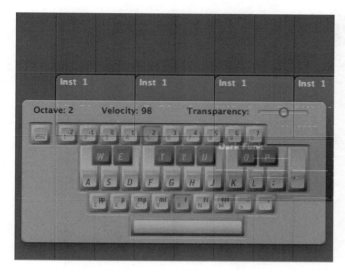

The Caps Lock keyboard

Navigation by Marker

Markers could become your pride and joy in Logic. They are the key to keeping a song arrangement well organized, and a brilliant navigation tool. There are key commands to jump to the next and previous marker (Go to Next Marker, Go to Previous Marker). These create your visual road map of the Logic project arrangement. Markers are generally used to designate the main structural sections of your Logic project. If it's a song, you can label the traditional sections of Introduction, Verse, Chorus, Verse 2, Bridge, Chorus 2, Break, Chorus Out, Ending, and so on. If you're a composer, use markers to specify all the related compositional sections of Introduction, Theme, Interlude, and so on.

- Creating markers in the global tracks

    Global tracks are, just as they sound, specialized tracks in Logic that contain data that applies uniformly to all the audio and MIDI tracks. The global tracks are found at the top of the track list, with a small disclosure triangle that opens the view to the various global tracks. Click on the global tracks to reveal the Marker track.

Global tracks

Now click on the disclosure triangle next to Marker track to open up the full view of creating, naming, and editing your Marker track.

Full view Marker track

Move the playhead to the point at which you'd like to create a marker, and hit the Create button in the Marker track header field.

The Create Marker button

You can adjust the start and end point of the marker by dragging on it. The Pointer tool turns into a bracket-shaped tool to make adjustments to the marker length, once you have at least two markers in the Marker track.

• Naming markers

Double-click into the marker to change its name from the default of Marker 1, Marker 2, and so on.

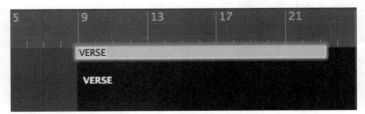

Naming markers

- Cycle by marker

  There are great ways to navigate quickly by your markers. There are key commands (covered in chapter 6, "The Secret to Learning Logic: Key Commands") that can be assigned to Go To Next Marker and Go To Previous Marker so you can quickly jump from Verse 1 to Chorus 2. When cycle is enabled in the Transport and the Marker track is in view in the global tracks, drag up on the marker into the bar ruler and the marker area will become the cycle area.

- View markers in the bar ruler

  After the Marker track is created, you can leave it in view or collapse it and then the markers will remain visible but smaller inside the bottom half of the bar ruler. You can't cycle by marker if the Marker track isn't in view, but you can use the Next/Previous key commands to fly between the markers.

Marker view in the bar ruler

- Coloring markers

  My secret pleasure is coloring markers: picking a color scheme that reflects the mood of the project and just looks good. Option + C will open the same color palette used for coloring tracks. Or, select the color palette in the toolbar. Simply click on the marker with your Pointer tool so that it's highlighted, then select the color in the color palette you'd like to assign.

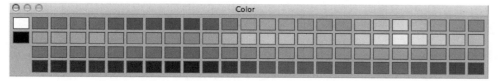

The Color Palette

Hiding Tracks You Don't Need to See

Another handy navigation tool is the ability to limit or hide what's in view in the Arrange window so you can navigate quickly around tracks and regions you need to focus on.

There are two steps to hiding tracks. First enable the Hide button in the toolbar, right above the track list in the Arrange window. The icon on the Hide button is an "H". When selected, it glows a bright lime green and an "H" button appears on all of the track headers in the track list to the left of the Record Enable button.

Now, click on the Hide button on each of the tracks that you don't want in view. The track can be muted or unmuted so that it plays back even while hidden. Once all the tracks are identified, hit the "H" button again in the toolbar, and all the selected tracks will be removed from view in the Arrange window. The Hide button now turns orange, indicating that there are hidden tracks. The Hide button is a toggle. Hit it again, and the hidden tracks will be back in view.

Track Hide in the toolbar

This is very handy if you don't need to see a group of tracks that may not be part of the final arrangement but you don't want to delete them, or if you just want a tidy workspace (especially when it's a large project). While you're mixing all 24 vocal tracks, you may not want your visual focus to be distracted by all the orchestral, synth, or drum parts.

Be careful—it's easy to forget about tracks that you've hidden and then get confused looking at your Logic project. The orange glow on the Hide button is your reminder. However, you may still find yourself wondering what on earth you're hearing, when it's just a group of tracks you hid but didn't mute last week.

Navigating in the Browser

The entire section of the Arrange window on the right is truly powerful. It is revealed and collapsed by clicking on the Media area button in the upper right.

The Media area of the Arrange window

Very few Logic users verbally reference the Media area, but the tabs within are very familiar friends. Here, you have access to all the content that came with Logic as well as the content that you create, as far as Apple Loops, channel strip settings, and the Audio Bin for each Logic project. Further, you can navigate to all the Logic projects on your hard drive, and to connected drives from here. This is useful if you need to bring in a random audio file on your drive or, as you'll see in the next section on Track Import, import all the settings and assets from another project.

Track Import

From the Browser tab, you can navigate to any Logic project to import elements from it. When you find the project folder, double-click on the Logic song file within it. Once the project is visible in the Browser view, you will see a complete table of all the assets from that project (that is, audio tracks, software instrument tracks, and even auxiliary tracks. Here you can enable and disable any of the tracks and their associated components, and then select on the bottom to add or replace that track in the Arrange workspace. In other words, take everything or one individual component like the plug-in chain from a really hot bass line or the MIDI from a killer drum groove you programmed. This is also a great starting point for creating a remix by grabbing the vocal tracks and placing them in an empty project.

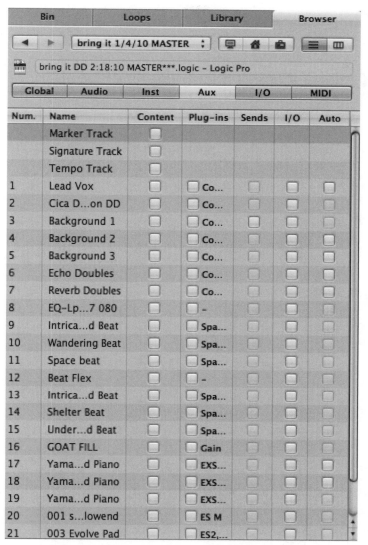

The Track Import table

There are two rows of labels in the Track Import window, the one on top referring to the type of track (whether audio, instrument, auxiliary, MIDI, and so on). This allows you to focus on which tracks you need to import if you're working on a large project. The columns beneath in the Track Import window are as follows:

- Track Numbers: The track numbers in the track list of the Arrange window.
- Track Names: The track names as labeled in the track list of the Arrange window.
- Content: The MIDI or audio data contained on a selected track. All the regions in the Arrange workspace. These can be imported independently of the plug-in chain on the track.
- Plug-ins: Self-explanatory, here you elect to include the entire plug-in chain from a track, including third-party plug-ins.
- Sends: This will include the bus assignments on the ends. This field will be grayed out if there are no Send assignments on the track.
- Auto: The automation data on the track.

Note: You cannot import track data from an open Logic project. Logic does allow you to have more than one project open at a time, so you may accidentally catch yourself trying to import data from a project that's open!

Global Tab: Importing Tempo, Signature, and Markers

This tab may not be enabled by default. Click on it if you want to import the Tempo, Signature, and/or Marker track data, the information stored in the global tracks in the Arrange window.

Global	Audio	Inst	Aux	I/O	MIDI

Num.	Name	Content	Plug-ins	Sends	I/O	Auto
	Marker Track	☐				
	Signature Track	☐				
	Tempo Track	☐				
1	Lead Vox	☐	☐ Co...	☐	☐	☐

Global tracks import

Import Project Settings

This is not something I've ever needed, but you might. You can independently import the Settings from the session, from Tuning to Metronome Settings. Select the Import Settings button at the bottom of the screen, and a dialog box will open in which you can check off the components you're interested in using for different recording setups.

Import Settings

☐ Screensets	☐ Transform Sets	☐ Hyper Sets
☐ Score Sets	☐ Staff Styles	☐ Text Styles
☐ Score Settings		
☐ Sync Settings	☐ Metronome Settings	☐ Record Settings
☐ Tuning Settings	☐ Audio Settings	☐ Midi Settings
☐ Video Settings	☐ Asset Settings	

(Cancel) (Import)

Import project settings

Editing in Logic

Editing in Logic, especially audio, is greatly misunderstood. The Logic MIDI editing is, of course, deeply respected for its depth; the audio editing, however, is more of an acquired appreciation.

It Starts and Ends in the Arrange Window

The Arrange window is your starting point for moving MIDI and audio data around; it is where you create your project arrangement and where you do the majority of your work. Here you move around musical objects called *regions*, which (as previously introduced) are the fundamental building blocks of your Logic project. A region is a container for either MIDI note events or a piece of an audio recording.

Here are a few basics of Arrange window region editing:

- Copy Region: Either Option-drag, or drag the upper right corner to the right with the Region Looping tool.
- Repeat Regions/Events (by a user-specified number of bars): Press the Command + R key.
- Mute Notes/Region: Press the "M" key.
- Solo Notes/Region: Press the "S" key.
- Highlight a region, and then Ctrl + Shift + Drag: Move/Nudge by a *tick* (the smallest increment of a beat, or 1/3,840 of a beat).
- Cut Region: Marquee-select then click with Pointer tool.

Power Tip: The Tick, the Smallest Nudge Value

A bit of trivia: the value of a *tick*, 1/3,840 of a beat, didn't come out of thin air: the standard for hardware sequencers became 960 ppqn (pulses per quarter note) after the original 96 ppqn of early sequencers in the '80s.

Piano Roll MIDI Editing

A whole book could easily be written on the editing available in the Piano Roll. This editor was integral to the original power of Logic for songwriters and composers.

Note Position and Length: Select and drag a MIDI note event up, down, left, or right to adjust its position. As soon as you highlight a MIDI note, a help tag appears with the exact position in the timeline. Use the Pencil tool from the local Tool menus or the Escape key to create a new note event. To adjust the note length, drag on the right edge of a note event and pull left or right. The Pointer tool switches from an arrow to a bracket shape indicating that the note length will be adjusted and the help tag reinforces by indicating the amount of the length change. Grab any green Apple Loop or record a few MIDI notes, then experiment with these fantastic tools.

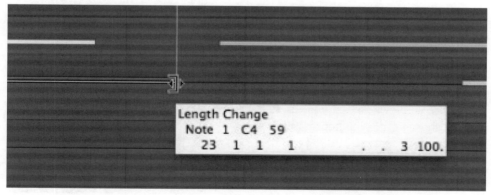

Note Length change

Velocity Edits: Logic provides great visual indication of the velocity levels with color, red signifying the loudest and blue the quietest. When you drag up or down with the Velocity tool (labeled with a small "V"), accessed from the Tool menu, the note changes color while the help tag gives you the exact velocity level on the scale between 0 and 127.

Quantize Edits: Quantizing in the Piano Roll editor is very satisfying. Grab the Quantize tool from the Tool menu or the Escape key labeled with a "Q", and then select a single note or a group of notes. A pull-down menu will appear to select the quantization value of all highlighted notes.

Power Tip: Silent Edits with the MIDI Out Button

This is extremely helpful. If you disable the MIDI Out button, you will not hear any note events selected in the Piano Roll. This is a great feature to adjust depending on the situation. For example, say you are blasting a track in your speakers with other people vibing in the studio when you realize that the kick velocities need to be adjusted. If you disable the MIDI Out, no one has to listen while you drag the velocity levels around and hear a barrage of kick hits. You can drag on the note events with the Velocity tool and use the help tag for visual feedback of your adjustment.

Disable the MIDI Out button for silent edits

Linking Editor Windows

The chain link icon in the upper left of most windows is very handy. When it is enabled, the button glows and the two active windows will be linked, meaning that what you do in one window will be directly connected to the content of the linked window. For example, when the Score Editor has the link enabled, whichever MIDI track in the Arrange window is highlighted will be visible in the Score Editor, even while you are recording.

That's usually fantastic, but there are situations in which you may prefer to look at the Score data from another track. If you're going to rip a solo to follow a chord progression you just played on another instrument, you may want to unlink the windows so that you can follow the notated chords while you improvise.

Very Important Editing Preferences

There are a lot of great editing preferences, and how you assign them is definitely a matter of taste. From Preferences in the toolbar, select General and then Editing. A few of the most notable preferences are listed below.

Linked Editors

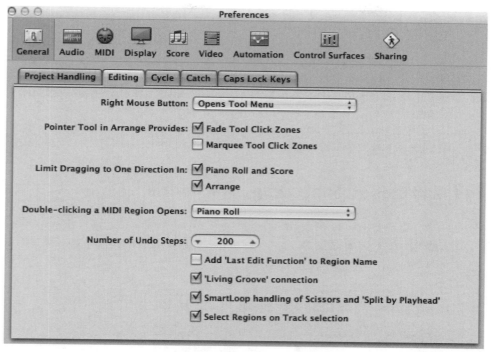

Editing preferences

- Right mouse button: Assign the right-click of your mouse to a third tool. This sort of navigation is generally considered convenient to PC users.
- Pointer tool in the Arrange window: Fade tool and Marquee tool click zones can be introduced to the Pointer tool's functionality. I recommend experimenting here to see if they work for you. The Fade Tool Click Zone assignment is very slick and allows you to simply swipe across the upper right or left of a region to create a fade.

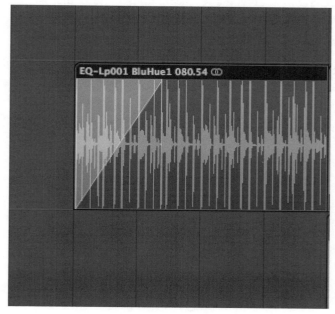

Fade Tool Click Zone

With Marquee Tool Click Zone enabled, your Pointer tool will switch to the Marquee tool in the lower half of a region.

Limit Dragging to One Direction In…: You may find this valuable to enable in the Arrange window as well as in Score and in Piano Roll. Generally, when moving regions around you will be moving them either forward or backward in the timeline and you don't want them to slip to the track below or above. Similarly, if I'm moving data up or down to another track, I don't want it to move forward or back in the timeline.

Double-clicking on a MIDI region opens: You may want to leave this on Piano Roll. If you're a composer or a more traditional musician, you may prefer the Score or Event List to open here.

Edit Grid Menus: Snap, Drag, and Shuffle

This feature throws a lot of users off, so read carefully and then explore on your own. The Edit modes in the upper right corner of the Arrange window determine how regions will behave when you move them around, especially if you move them on top of one another.

Snap and Drag

The Drag menu determines the behavior of regions in the Arrange window. The default is Overlap.

Power Tip: Switch to No Overlap as Default

I recommend switching to No Overlap in the Drag menu. This is the standard mode in Pro Tools and forces regions to replace each other when one is placed on top of the other. When you are editing audio, any region underneath another audio file will be eliminated.

Shuffle Right and Shuffle Left are self-explanatory. When enabled, regions will behave like magnets, butting up to the region to the right or left, depending whether Shuffle Right or Shuffle Left is selected.

The X-Fade mode allows for automatic crossfades between regions, which can be convenient. This will create an automatic crossfade when two regions overlap as the result of an edit.

The Snap modes determine the division Logic regions snap to when editing, whether Bar, Beat, Division, Tick (1/3,840 of a beat) or the default on top, which is Smart Snap. This is dependent on your zoom level and is the best choice 90 percent of the time, unless you're performing a specific edit task requiring regions to move by a designated amount, such as by a beat or a bar.

Chapter 6
THE SECRET TO LEARNING LOGIC: KEY COMMANDS

Key commands are the essence of both learning Logic and working with speed and efficiency as a power Logic user. If you have not yet spent much time in Key Commands window, start doing so immediately. Give yourself adequate time to explore this vast universe of more than 1,000 keyboard shortcuts in Logic, not just while you are in the heat of writing, but also allow quality study time to learning Logic. Remember, Logic is now your instrument, and you must practice.

To access the Key Commands window, go to the Preference button in the toolbar then select Key Commands from the bottom of the list (Preferences > Key Commands). Or, open the window from a key command. The default is Option + K.

Make time to read through the functions listed in the Key Commands window. If you don't understand exactly what one means, assign it to a key and try to test it out. It's a great tool in your discovery process of what's possible with Logic and becoming a power Logic user.

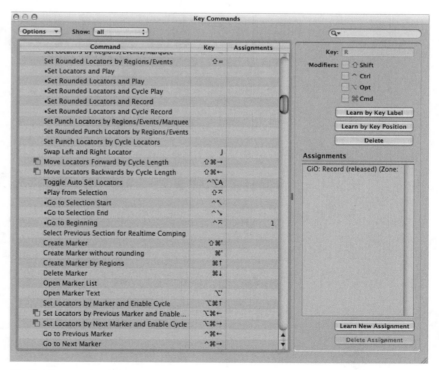

The Key Commands window

Creating Custom Key Commands

To modify an existing key command, enable the "Learn by Key Label" button on the right. Next, use the search field in the upper right to navigate to the function you want to assign a keystroke to. Then select a key combination using a letter key with or without a modifier key.

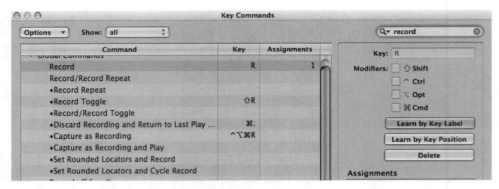

Assigning a key command

If the key combination is already in use, a dialog box will pop up telling you what the keystroke was previously assigned to. You'll have the option to override and replace its assignment or find another key combination. If you envision a keystroke for an action but it was in use and you didn't even know it, there's a good chance it was not an assignment you cared about. Whether you make a new assignment or decide to leave a previously assigned one, make the effort to use it right away to help commit it to memory.

Finding Out What a Key Command Is Assigned To

Simply hit the key or combination of key and modifier key, and the Key Commands window will jump to the assigned key command and it will be highlighted. Be sure that nothing is typed into the search field in the upper right of your screen or this won't work!

Loading Key Command Sets

You can access different key command sets from within the Key Commands window. This means that you can carry yours around to load in another studio. To load another key command set, select the Options menu in the upper left of the Key Commands window. Here you will find the factory presets including key commands in different languages. There is also a Pro Tools key command set that you may or may not find helpful if you are a Pro Tools user. Since many functions have different names in the two DAWs, the translation is a bit inexact.

Beneath the presets is the option to import and export your own key command set.

Export menu for your key commands

To save your customized key commands, use the Export function and they will be automatically saved to the key command subfolder within the Logic folder in your Home folder.

File path in Finder to key commands

Once you've created your own custom set, it will appear under the presets, below the divider line. If you are bringing your custom set to another studio, use the Import menu to navigate to your portable drive.

Printing (and Memorizing) the Key Commands

This is a highly recommended step on your road to becoming one with Logic. Under Options, select Copy Key Commands to Clipboard and then open Microsoft Word or another text edit application. Next select Paste or Command + V, and the key commands will be pasted into a document that you can now print.

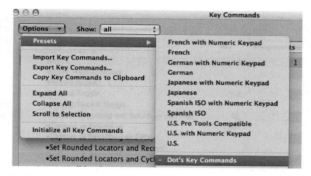

Dot's custom key commands

Before you copy to the clipboard, you may want to limit the key commands view to just the ones that are assigned, labeled Used in the Show menu to the right. Otherwise, the document you print out may be quite lengthy in order to accommodate more than 1,000 key commands.

Select used key commands

If you forget which symbol refers to the various modifier keys on the QWERTY keyboard like Ctrl or Option, there is a table in the upper right of the Key Commands window.

Power Tip: Protecting Your Key Commands

A common troubleshooting recommendation when Logic is acting buggy is to trash your Logic preferences. However, the key commands are actually stored in the Logic Preference file. They won't be deleted but you'll have to reload them from the Preset window. To avoid this extra step, under Preferences in the toolbar, there is an option halfway down the menu to initialize—trash—all preferences except your key commands.

Dot's Favorite Key Commands

Here's a confession. I have committed to memory only 30 or so key commands. But these alone provide me the speed and dexterity I encourage you to develop. Over the years, many Logic users watching me work have asked me to send them this list, which is shared in Appendix A.

Cross-reference in the book any terminology and features you are not familiar with. Now start your own hot list of key commands to commit to memory with any of mine you find relevant to your workflow. Your list should be a living document that you update and reference regularly, especially in the beginning. In actuality, new key commands are introduced relevant to new features with every new version of Logic. Your personal hot list of key commands should be revised accordingly. (See Appendix A for Dot's Top 30 Key Commands.)

General...
Audio...
MIDI...
Display...
Score...
Video...
Automation...
Sharing...

Initialize All Except Key Commands...
Audio Units Manager...
Chord Grid Library...

Control Surfaces...
Control Surfaces Setup...
Controller Assignments...

Key Commands...

Initializing preferences except your key commands

Chapter 7
CREATING WITH LOGIC'S SOFTWARE INSTRUMENTS

This chapter is at the heart and soul of Logic's significance in the history of music software. The palette of instruments that come with the Logic Studio software is truly vast and not fully appreciated by many newer Logic users who head straight to virtual instruments developed by other manufacturers. The entire suite of Logic instruments not only sound fantastic (especially when you develop the habit of layering with effects and saving them as channel strip settings), but they also perform with very low latency and maximum CPU efficiency—thanks to how tightly they are integrated into Logic's audio engine. This is the blessing and the curse of them ironically being available only within Logic, and not as Audio Units available in other Mac-based DAWs. To many musicians, it was a bit unfair for Apple to herald the Audio Unit plug-in format for OS X but not make their own Logic virtual instruments and effects plug-ins available as Audio Units. That's old news now and it's just lucky we're all Logic users here.

That is not to say that instruments by other manufacturers shouldn't be added to your palette, given how diverse and brilliant the options are today and that Logic is a great, stable Audio Unit host. The point is simply that the Logic palette should not be overlooked. These instruments are incredibly efficient within Logic. They load and play back quickly, and any manipulations will easily store with your Logic project. Get into the habit of tweaking a chain of plug-ins on top of the Logic instruments and save these as channel strip settings in folders relevant to you (for example, Pop Drum Kits, Fav Synths, Secret Sounds, and so on), and you'll have a palette of sounds like no one else in the world.

Uninitiated Logic users often load a Logic instrument the traditional way—in the input field of a software instrument track on the leftmost channel strip in the Arrange window. They scroll through its presets, and then come to the conclusion that the instrument is thin and boring. The richness of Logic instruments come to life when they are tweaked, layered with plug-ins, and saved as channel strip settings with a chain of effects in the pane at the top of the channel strip (described in detail just below). There is one important note, however. If you entered the world

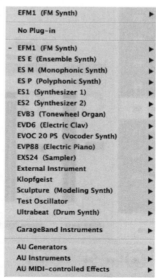

Loading an instrument into an I/O insert

of Logic and computer-based recording in recent years, without having grown up in the world of analog synthesis, my best advice is to read up as soon as possible on the fundamentals of sound synthesis in the analog world. It's fascinating science that will give you a broader appreciation of creating inside the computer. While many purists today swear by the sonic characteristics of analog synthesizers and modular synthesis, I believe you can achieve comparable results with virtual instruments and plug-ins by sheer experimentation after gaining an appreciation of the fundamentals. You'll also have the advantage in the digital world of being able to store, recall, and back up your settings—and always have them in tune, a big plus. In the days of the analog world, there was a fragility to the oscillators' vibration that almost seemed to depend on your remembering what shoes you were wearing when you created the sound and the exact mood in the studio in order for analog synth parts to sound the same from one day to the next.

Software instruments actually do a remarkable job of reproducing analog synthesis. To truly enjoy and get the most out of these algorithmic representations found in Logic, it helps to understand the fundamentals of oscillators, filters, LFO oscillators, and envelope generators, and sound design in the analog world. It's a brilliant mad science that is likely to inspire you and your music.

Loading, Tweaking, and Saving Channel Strip Settings

Channel strip settings were introduced in chapter 2's "Dual Channel Strip, Channel Strip Settings, and the Inspector" tour of the Arrange window and was later discussed in chapter 4's "Mixing Your Music" tour of the Mixer in the context of saving combinations of plug-in settings on an audio track. In this chapter we'll focus more on the channel strip settings for software instruments. Up to 16 plug-ins can be loaded on a software instrument track, just as with an audio track. If you need more processing than that on a single track, I'd recommend reconsidering your source audio or choice of software instrument.

The Settings Library

The Library is contextual. This means that a different menu of presets or settings is revealed depending what you select on the channel strip. Click on the Channel Strip Setting pane at the top of channel strip first—a white halo will appear around that pane. All of its possible channel strip settings are now in view in the Library.

Depending what type of track you have highlighted, you will see either Library settings for audio tracks or software instruments. Click once on any insert on the channel strip setting, and all the presets for that plug-in will be in view. The same thing happens with the software instrument input pane, lower down on the channel strip (EXS24, Sculpture, ES2, and so on) and directly above the output.

Contextual View of Library

The preset or channel strip setting in the Library is loaded by double-clicking on it. Press the Up Arrow or Down Arrow key to select the next or previous (or left or right) to move backward or forward through the categories. Try this now.

Making Your Own Channel Strip Settings

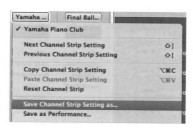

Clicking-and-holding the slot at the top of the channel strip reveals an additional hierarchical approach for selecting channel strips besides navigating in the Library. This is also where you can save your own channel strip settings. It is admittedly a bit confusing that you cannot save a channel strip setting anywhere in the Library to the right of the Arrange window. Once you understand the workflow, it becomes quite natural to save on the left on the channel strip itself, and then "shop" in the Library on the right.

Saving a channel strip setting

Power Tip: Navigating Quickly Through the Library

If you click on a category folder level in the Library of channel strip settings, it will reveal its contents in the column to the right. If you are all the way in the furthest-most column on the right viewing channel strip settings that are two folders deep (Voices > Warped Voices > Phone Filter), triple-clicking on a setting will take you back to the root folder level of channel strip settings instead of having to use the scrollbar at the bottom of the Library to back out.

Backing Up and Carrying Around Your Logic Instrument

Channel strip settings that you create are saved to your Home folder in this file path: Home > Library > Application Support > Logic > Channel Strip Settings

This Logic folder should be backed up regularly to another hard drive! Besides, if you have this Logic folder with you at all times on a portable drive, you are carrying your palette of plug-in and channel strip settings that should be part of your pride and creative arsenal as a professional Logic user—you will be carrying around your instrument. This will be discussed further in chapter 11, "Good Housekeeping and Other Smart Practices."

The EXS24 Sampler: The Workhorse of Logic

Over a decade ago, the EXS24 was one of the first virtual samplers on the market. It was introduced as an alternative to hardware-based samplers and was quite innovative for its time. The name EXS24 is an acronym for "extreme sampler," with the "24" meaning 24-bit resolution. Today, the EXS24 ships with a library of more than 1,300 sampled instruments. It is your most essential instrument in Logic.

The proposition of taking advantage of the enormous amount of RAM available to a computer as compared with a hardware-based sampler was quite powerful a decade ago. Coupled with the amount of hard-drive space that a computer offers as compared with standalone samplers, the EXS24 was the

The EXS24 Sampler Instrument

beginning of the digital sampling revolution. It sadly has not been updated as often since its introduction in 2000 as many Logic users would like. There are a number of virtual samplers that have been introduced since the EXS that run circles around its features and design. That said, there are three significant reasons that it should be a central part of your sample-based arsenal as a Logic user:

- #1: The EXS24 is highly efficient CPU-wise and incredibly stable within Logic. This means that you can have literally dozens of instances of it open without creating any system overloads. The sample editor inside the EXS24 is actually Logic's own audio editor—not a separate engine—and so the integration is tight.

- #2: The front end of the EXS has a powerful synthesizer including Logic's filter, which has been appreciated by old-school Logic users for years for its warmth and resonance. Tweaking your samples with the EXS filter and LFOs will easily achieve truly sonic results. Some examples are below under "Old-School Synth Features: Lowpass Filter and LFO Tricks."

Power Tip: EXS24 Samples in Your Project Folder

Be sure that both the EXS sampler instruments and the samples assets are specifically checked off inside your Logic project folder, or you will be wondering why you open a Logic project on another computer and the samples are missing!

EXS file management in Logic project

- #3: The sampler instrument and associated samples of an EXS instrument can automatically save to your Logic project folder when you save the project, as long as the two checkboxes are enabled to copy the EXS instrument and copy EXS samples to the project folder. This means that you will never show up in another studio without your favorite kick or snare. Specifically, the Include Assets subfolders must be checked when you save your Logic project. This way, you will always have the kick, snare, and string samples you need. With a third-party sampler (whether Battery, Kontakt, or otherwise), you need to remember to manually bring your folders of associated samples each time.

The easiest way to load a factory preset is from the Library. The EXS presets are automatically displayed when the software instrument insert on the channel strip is selected and the Library is open.

The more than 1,300 factory-sampled instruments are also accessed on the front panel of the EXS instrument plug-in by clicking-and-holding in the black area, where the dropdown menu is available. This is the old-school, clumsier way, compared with using the Library.

Loading factory EXS presets from the plug-in front panel

Drag-and-Drop Samples:
Creating Your Own EXS Instrument

Here are the steps to create your own EXS instrument from scratch.

- Select a new software instrument track from the Create Track menu at top of the track list. It will default to an EVP88 electric piano.
- Next, click-and-hold on the Input pane in the I/O area, directly above what is labeled Stereo Out on the channel strip to the left.
- Select the EXS from the list of instruments.
- Double-click to open the front panel of the instrument
- A new EXS24 instrument is created automatically, loaded as the preset, and generically named instrument #456, and so on.
- Rename your new EXS instrument in the local Edit menu (Instrument > Save As).

The I/O pane on the channel strip

Editor view of a new EXS instrument

- Here, drag-and-drop any audio file onto the key in the virtual keyboard where you want the sample to be triggered.
- Set the range by dragging left and right.
- You can drag multiple samples at once. A dialog box opens asking how you want the samples to be placed. Experiment with all the options to pick the one appropriate to how you want the samples to be layered.

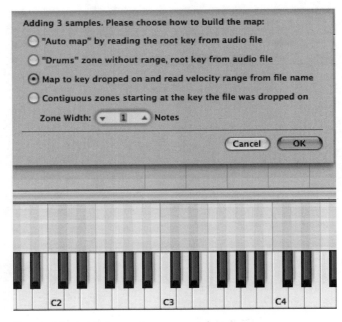

Drag and Drop multiple samples

When you add a sample, a zone is created that contains the parameters of the sample (such as pitch, key range, volume, or pan). To apply edits to multiple zones at once, you can organize zones into groups: Select Group > New Group. Then name the group in the left column. Click-and-drag in the Editor to select the zones you want to add into the group folder.

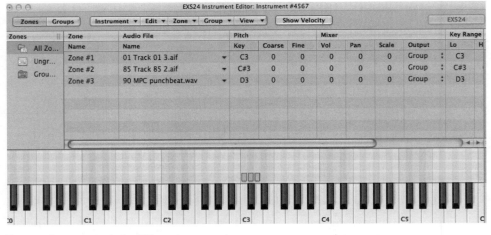

Zones and zone groups in the EXS

Old-School Synth Features: Lowpass Filter and LFO Tricks

The main EXS24 window looks like a classic virtual analogue synth, with envelope generators for filter and amplitude, a resonant filter, and two LFOs for modulation. The filter has four modes from 12 to 24 dB slopes to experiment with (with Fat or Classic 24 dB settings), along with resonance and distortion options. The two LFOs (low frequency oscillators) each have a range of waveforms that can be synced to Logic's tempo for classic pulsing analog effects. Unlike a virtual synthesizer, the sound source in the EXS24 is not an oscillator but a sampled "instrument" in your Library.

Technically speaking, the EXS24 is a sample-playback instrument. Any sample recording and much of the sample editing is done directly in Logic. The edited sound can then be triggered in the EXS24 simply by loading it into a zone.

The LFO1 and LFO2 are perfect for quick, creative pulsing effects. To appreciate any virtual instrument, it's important to understand the LFO building block in the analog synthesizer world. The acronym LFO stands for "low-frequency oscillator" and refers to an oscillator that is not directly audible, cycling at a frequency below 20 Hz, but is useful for creating rhythmic pulses and modulating effects on the main sound sources or oscillators. These are one of the fundamental stages of modular synths. Like standard oscillator circuits that generate sound in a synthesizer, they may be one of a number of waveforms, such as sine, square, sawtooth, and so on.

Here are the easy steps to start experimenting with the LFO, ideally on a synth pad type of sound.

To Do:

- Choose New Track > Load software instrument.
- Click-and-hold on the I/O Input insert on the new channel strip defaulting to EVP88 to select the EXS24 from the Instrument menu.
- Select the EXS24 in Stereo.
- From the Library on the right of EXS settings, select the Synthesizers folder, and then Synth Pads. Click to load Basic Pad.
- Assign the LFO 2 Rate to 1/8 in the bottom row of the interface by dragging on the knob or double-clicking on the value beneath the knob.
- In the Modulation Matrix directly above, assign one router's Destination to Cutoff and the Source to LFO2, and the "via" setting in the middle to velocity or pitch bend.
- Experiment with the LFO2 Rate (with 1/16, 1/32, 1/4, and so on) and listen to the pulse speed up and slow down in time with your Logic project.
- Add an Apple Loop or program a drumbeat to test the LFO sync within the Logic project.

Pulsing FX with LFO 2 and the modulation matrix

File Management of Your EXS24 Library

It is very easy and practical to develop a massive EXS24 Library. Aside from building your own sampled instruments, there are literally hundreds of native EXS24 libraries available from other manufacturers, as well as being able to read Giga and Akai format. This means your EXS24 Library will easily contain every kind of drum kit, natural and electronic, every type of sound from the fat analog to the pure orchestral instrument, for every genre of music.

You do have to understand the basic file hierarchy. The EXS Library consists of two folders: the Sampler Instruments and the associated Samples. The sampler instruments, which have the extension ".exs" at the end of their file name, take up very little drive space. These are the mappings of the instrument whose file size can be as small as 3 kB or 4 kB (maybe up to 30 kB or 40 kB), while the associated samples will add up quickly to massive gigabytes of data.

Aside from creating your own drum kits, a great project is to create an EXS instrument with unique sound effects you collect that will be your "go to" folder for adding accents to your session.

Power Tip: Where Are Your Samples?

The samples can be stored anywhere on your hard drive or external hard drives. Just be sure to always have that drive nearby or take the time to at least copy the samples of your favorite sampler instruments to your internal drive (maybe the main 25 to 30 instruments of drum kits, synths, strings, and so on). Your "go-to" sampler instruments and their samples will likely not take up more than a few gigabytes and will easily fit on your internal drive.

The Sampler Instruments folder must be in your Logic folder within your Home folder, or at least an alias of them must be in that location. To create an alias, Ctrl-click on the Sampler Instrument folder from the Finder view and select Make Alias.

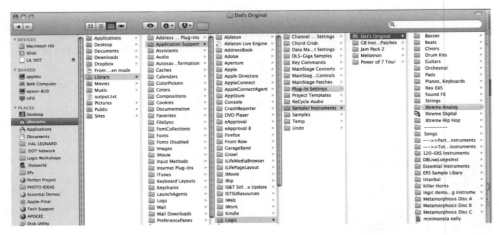

The Finder view of your EXS Library

An EXS Trick: Sample Group Key Switching

The EXS can re-create acoustic and orchestral instruments with unbelievable realism and real-time control. There is a great feature in the EXS for switching between sample groups by hitting either a foot pedal or a mod wheel, or even using the keys in the lowest register of the keyboard to trigger different sample groups assigned to the same key, recorded as a different type of performance. For example, a Bösendorfer piano made up of almost 4 gigabytes of samples may use the sustain pedal to switch between two discrete sets of samples. A violin sampler library could trigger pizzicato, legato, or even trill strings from the same keyboard zones by sample group switching, maybe activated from one register of keys on the keyboard, in the low or high range. Or, velocity may be used on a nylon guitar patch to select a sample with a string slide.

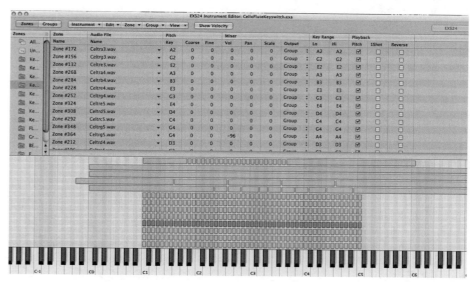

Sample group switching

Power Tip: AutoSampling Your Hardware Synths

Autosampling your hardware synths and samplers is one of the most liberating projects you can schedule into your music life. There is a third-party product called AutoSampler, by Redmatica, that will read and sample all the sounds from your hardware synths and format them as EXS instruments. All you do is cable the synth's audio output to your audio interface and send MIDI cable bidirectionally to a MIDI interface connected to your computer. The results are remarkable, creating a functional backup for your mobile studio rig or live performances. You can specify exactly which notes will be sampled, and even sample every note at different velocity levels. After it samples, it will build the EXS instrument and place it in the directory you choose.

Once auto-sampled, big thick analog synth pads actually use very little CPU power. There's something astonishing about sitting on your couch listening to AutoSampler trigger each key on your keyboard, as though there were a ghost in the studio, or better yet, a fantasy studio intern. The resulting reproduction of the keyboard sounds in the EXS24 is uncanny. This feature is utilized by many major touring bands as the backup for when a keyboard goes down at an inopportune time.

The Futuristic ES2 Synth

It wouldn't be right to introduce the ES2 without first paying homage to its predecessor, the ES1, Logic's very first virtual instrument. This retro, monophonic virtual synth is still untouchable for fat, warm analog bass and synth sounds. Any serious Logic user knows this. In fact, the entire ES synth series deserves at least a mention. In addition to the ES1 and ES2, three other compact, no frills synths slipped into early Logic: ES P, ES E, and ES M. They have classic analog sounds without a lot of parameters to adjust, but you'll have great results manipulating the Cutoff and Resonance alone on their filters with just a bit of experimentation.

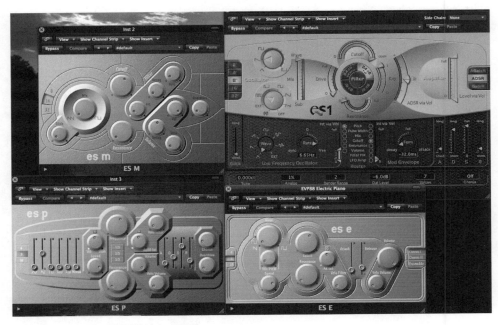

Early ES synths: ES1, ES P, ES M, and ES E

And then came the ES2 with its uncanny resemblance to the control panel of a sci-fi spaceship. It can be a bit overwhelming at first as far as where to focus your eye. Follow along on this tour of the main areas of its interface, and its massive palette of sound will become more accessible.

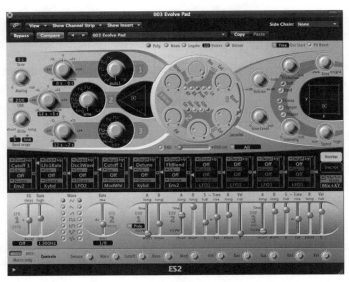

The futuristic ES2

At the upper left are the ES2's three impressive digital oscillators, the fundamental sound generators of a synthesizer. You can individually turn on or off each one by clicking on the lime-green number to the right of each oscillator. In the figure below, Oscillator 1 and 2 are enabled, and Oscillator 3 is disabled.

ES2 Oscillators with Osc 3 disabled

The experience of disabling an oscillator is quite visual on the ES2. You watch a transparent door "close" the oscillator. On each oscillator you dial up the desired waveform that is graphically indicated: sine, square, sawtooth, and so on. Another cool adjustment is made inside the black triangle, positioned between the three oscillators. Experiment with the blend of these three oscillators by dragging on the green vortex at the center of the triangle. As you make adjustments, the percentage of each oscillator is displayed and the character of sound shifts.

The ES2 oscillator blend

In the upper center area of the interface are the two self-resonating filters. One feature of all of Logic plug-ins is an incredibly warm and resonant filter, well known to any old-school Logic user. Experiment with the cutoff and resonance knobs for instant gratification of finding a sound that blends into your project.

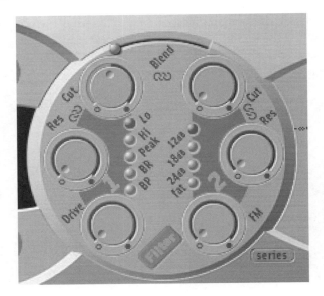

The ES2 filters

Edgy FX with the Randomizer

This is great fun for adding an edgy texture to your synth sounds. Beneath the two filters you'll find the randomizing section. There is a menu to the right where you select which elements to randomize (whether filters, envelopes, waveforms, and so on) and a slider to determine the intensity of randomization. The tiny button to the left triggers the randomization, and then an aggressive, analog growl is all yours.

ES2 Randomizer

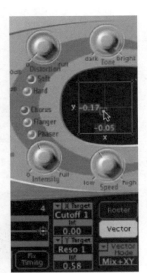

Planar Pad sweeping

X-Y Vector Pad Sweeping

The Planar Pad is like a mini Korg Kaoss Pad for the ES2, with a retro *x-y* touchpad MIDI controller in the upper right of the interface. To assign parameters to the two axes below in the Router section, first switch the active tab from Router to Vector and then choose from the menu which parameters you'd like the *x*-axis and the *y*-axis to control. Start with Cutoff 2 and Resonance 2, since they are easy to hear and are sonically pleasing, if you like big analog sweeping effects.

ES2 Modulation Matrix

This is a chapter in and of itself. Suffice to say, you can assign the matrix to Router or Vector mode. The Router mode is similar to that of the EXS24 for creating rich modulating effects. The Vector mode gets interesting. Shift-click to create nodes that will impact the trajectory of the sound in time.

Ultrabeat: Unlocking the Beat Machine and Drum Sampler

Many Logic users overlook the power of the Ultrabeat drum machine in the Logic instrument collection. It combines a variety of ways to generate your drum sounds: virtual analog, FM, component modeling (like Sculpture), and sample playback like the EXS24. Ultrabeat is sometimes stereotyped as only "electronic kits for dance music," when in fact there are masterfully sampled natural kits such as the Indie Live Kit and Studio Brush Kit. Further, you can directly import EXS24 drum kits. That means taking advantage of the unique Ultrabeat synthesizer engine and step sequencer with your full EXS Library.

A great way to begin discovering Ultrabeat's power by loading one of the factory drum kits, and then trying out the factory built-in patterns in the step sequencer at the bottom of the interface.

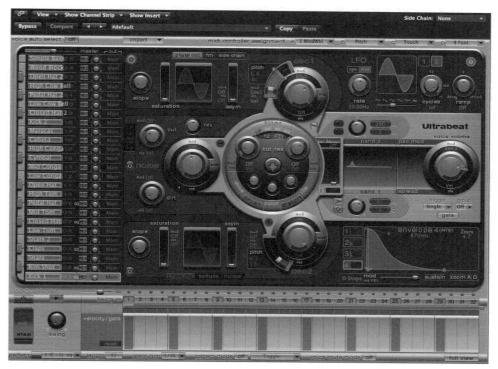

The Ultrabeat interface

Quick Tour of the Drum Module

Each of the 25 drum sounds in a kit has its own individual sound parameters that can be independently adjusted in the drum synthesizer section in the middle. This is what makes Ultrabeat such a powerful drum module: it is 25 separate instruments in the kit. As you play each drum sound, you will see Ultrabeat's interface change to display the parameters of that selected drum sound. Watch how the parameters' settings change as you switch to a different drum sound.

Power Tip: Voice Auto Select

Enable the Voice Auto Select button near the top of the interface above the Mixer section so that the interface updates as you select a different drum sound.

The Voice Auto Select button

The individual drum sounds and mixer section are on the left of the interface. Once the Voice Auto Select is enabled, click on the small music keyboard to the far left of the drum sounds to preview them, or trigger from a MIDI controller keyboard. Dragging the blue bar further to the right will make that drum sound louder; to decrease volume, drag to the left and shorten the blue bar. Mute, Solo, and Pan switches are to the right of each drum sound. The output assignments are in the final column on the right of the mixer section. Click-and-hold to assign past the Main Outs to Outputs 3–4, 5–6, and so on.

The Drum Synthesizer in Ultrabeat

On the right is the crazy drum synthesizer section that will make a lot of sense in a minute. Focus your eye first on the three circular sound generators that can be individually enabled for whichever drum is highlighted in the Mixer. Two are oscillators, and the one in the middle is a noise generator. To enable or disable, click on the small circle to the left of each sound generator. It will turn red when enabled. In the illustration below, Oscillator 1 and the noise generator are enabled. Oscillator 2 is not.

Ultrabeat's drum sounds and mixer

All of the sound generators feed in the center to the Filter, the large circular section in the middle of the interface. The Filter section also includes Logic's very popular Bitcrusher and Distortion effects to give your drum sounds a real bite. Enable the link from each sound generator to the Filter with the small circles pointing toward it. They turn red when enabled.

Just by playing with the mix of sound generators and routing to the Filter—tweaking its cutoff and resonance and then the drive, distortion, and

Enabling a sound generator

Bitcrusher—you'll find yourself quickly making useful adjustments to the drum sounds' character.

The Ultrabeat filter

Let's do an experiment so that you can hear all this.
- Load the Hip-Hop '90s kit.
- Highlight the snare in the Mixer, the third instrument from the bottom.
- By default, the snare sound is being generated by Oscillator 2 and the Noise Generator in the middle.
- Increase the gain with the center knob of the Noise Generator. Try fully rotating it to full gain.
- Turn on the link to the Filter.
- Now enable and disable each sound generator individually.
- To adjust the level of each sound generator, select the inner circle and adjust the level of the red semicircular bar. Its Gain level appears in decibels in a small info bar as you adjust.

Snare sound experiment

When you're feeling your inner tweakhead, there are great effects on the right side of the Ultrabeat interface, including a Ring Modulator, EQ section, Pan Modulator, and Stereo Spread, an LFO, and four assignable envelopes. At the bottom is an ambitious step sequencer, which will be covered next.

The Step Sequencer

Ultrabeat is also a full-fledged drum machine by virtue of the 32-step sequencer at the bottom of the interface. The 32-step sequencer allows you to program Ultrabeat like a vintage drum machine step sequencer. It's very easy to program and it's fun. There are 24 patterns per drum kit, selected right here in the bottom left. The letters "SQ" mean the pattern has data. Ctrl-click to clear a pattern.

The Pattern list

What's fantastic about using the step sequencer is that you can take an old-school approach to drum programming, then just drag the MIDI data to the Arrange window so it's integrated into your project. We'll do that in a minute.

There are factory patterns to get you started that are visible in the lower left next to the step grid; the default pattern is labeled (C-1) sq.

As you choose each voice, you see the steps already entered and can enter new steps by just clicking on them. You can also drag across the small bar on top where the numbers are to enter a series of step events. Be careful—Ultrabeat can be playing even when Logic is not, which can sometimes throw you off.

Programming Hi-Hats

Once a voice is selected, drag across the keyboard or click directly on the step numbers above the keyboard to light up the steps to trigger the sound. Start by selecting a Hi-Hat in your drum kit.

Ultrabeat Trick #1: Humanizing the Feel

Drag the mouse across multiple steps of the Hi-Hat to select it. Then right click or Ctrl-click in the step grid area to randomize the velocity or gate time to enhance the groove and create a human drummer feel. Add an accent to any of the steps and individually control which voices get a swing feel. The amount of swing is controlled with the Swing knob. Switch Trigger mode to sustain.

Ultrabeat Trick #2: Deep Kicks with Envelope Controls

The Envelope Controls on the right of the interface, above the step grid, provide precise control over the Attack and Decay of notes to soften the Kick attack, for example. Switch on the Gate, then the length of the entered steps control the length of each note giving your kicks that deep *doom* sound.

First let's get set up. A pattern can be any length of up to 32 steps. Drag the blue bar right above the steps to adjust the pattern length.

The Full View of the Step Grid

Click on the Full View button in the lower right of the screen to enable Full View. Here, you can see and edit all the patterns for the instruments in your drum kit at once.

Triggering Vocal Samples in the Step Sequencer

The second oscillator can be used to trigger samples, and is normally used for short drum samples like kicks or snares. Take a look at what happens when you throw a longer sample in there, like a vocal or even spoken word. Grab any one of the Vocal Apple Loops that appeals to you. Drag it from the Apple Loop browser directly here to make it the sample triggered by Oscillator 2. We can reverse it, but not yet! Let's turn on the sequencer and enable a step in the step grid to trigger the sample. Simple enough. Here's where it gets interesting. If I drag this control element labeled "MAX" to a different portion of the region, it triggers the sample from that point—when I play at maximum velocity. Playing with a lower velocity will trigger the sample somewhere earlier in the file. If you experiment with dropping in steps with varying velocity and length, you're likely to quickly get some cool results.

Power Tip: Empty Kit to Load Sampler Instruments

There is a Drag-and-Drop sample kit that is not only emptied of any factory samples, but all the other oscillators and the link to the filter is disabled. This is important to know so that a fresh sample you load won't accidentally be filtered without your realizing it.

Ultrabeat Trick #3: Step Sequencer and Vocal Samples

- Copy a voice and its sequence.
- Paste both to another drum voice.
- Reverse the sample playback on the second voice in Osc 2.

- Pan the original and the copied voice each hard left and hard right.
- Shift the second sequence a few steps to the right by Option-clicking directly on the numbers.

Ultrabeat Trick #4: Adjusting the LFO

To add even more interest, experiment with the parameters of Osc 1. It's currently set to Phase Osc, so we just hear a basic sine wave tone—here's where we turn up the gain. We can adjust the shape or the pitch of the waveform with these controls (the slope, saturation, asymmetry). If you select LFO 1 under modulation for pitch and then spread the controls out, you hear the result immediately. Listen as you change the rate or shape of the LFO.

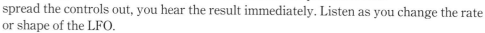

Copy/Paste drum voice and sequence

You can also switch the oscillator to FM. In this mode Oscillator 2, which is now the vocal sample, will modulate the sine wave of Oscillator 1. Increasing the amount of modulation can get extreme quickly, so play around and then disable Osc 1.

Dragging Step Sequencer Pattern to Arrange Window

You can pull the pattern out of the step sequence so it is MIDI data in the Arrange pattern by selecting the grid next to the Pattern button in the lower left of the screen. A help tag pops up saying, Drag to Arrange Window.

You'll see the MIDI notes from the Ultrabeat sequence. Then you can split them apart into independent regions based on the note pitch using the MIDI menu option Separate MIDI Events By Note Pitch, introduced in chapter 3, "Writing Your First Track in Logic." You can now easily build the arrangement by muting or otherwise changing each element of the kit separately with any of Logic's region parameters from velocity to gate time.

Drag pattern to Arrange

Import Alternate Kit and EXS Kit

The Import menu above the Mixer section has two killer functions. By default it opens a menu to view all the Ultrabeat kits. Here, you can select one to load as an alternate kit. This way you can drag a single drum element from the alternate kit directly into a slot of a drum sound from the main kit you're working with to replace it. Maybe you like the Hip-hop Heavy Kit, but want to use a kick from the Old School Funk Remix Kit.

Also, this same Import menu can be used to navigate to your full EXS24 Library of drum kits. You will breathe new life into the your EXS Library by viewing them inside the newer Ultrabeat interface, with options like easily reversing samples, and so on.

Import alternate or EXS kit

Sculpture's Otherworldly and Cinematic Sounds

Sculpture is referred to as a *component-modeling* or a *physical-modeling* synthesizer, which loosely means that it mathematically reproduces how sound is generated in the real world. Soon into experimenting with this virtual synthesizer, you will discover you have the ability to create otherworldly stringed instruments and highly atmospheric sounds. Sculpture shines at stringed and plucked sounds as well as complex textures that evolve over time.

The Basic String Section, the Pickup, and Exciters

Specifically Sculpture is re-creating what happens when a string is made to vibrate. The string is visible in the upper left hand side of the screen. Play any note now, and watch the string vibrate.

You change how the string is set into vibration using any of the three Exciters. Select either Strike, Pick, Bow, Blow, and so on, from the menu next to each Object. When you move the Pickup slider, you control where on the string it is acted upon. Just like with a real instrument, the timbre is quite different when you play near the bridge or play toward the middle of the string.

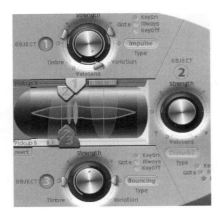

The String, the Pickup section, and the Exciters

The Material Pad

In the middle of the interface is a truly creative and fun stage of sculpting your sound. The Material Pad allows you to change the stiffness and absorption qualities of the virtual string, effectively transforming it from "steel" to "nylon" to "glass" and even "wood." You will hear the different materials as you manipulate the pad. Feel free to experiment now with one of the Atmosphere or Ambient Drone presets.

Reminder: Click on the Sculpture I/O insert on the channel strip, and its presets should be visible in the Library on the left of the Arrange window.

The Material Pad of the String

EQ and Physical Body of the Instrument

In this section on the right you have the ability to select the body of your virtual instrument, whether it's that of a ukulele or a double bass, which will change how much tension is placed on the instrument's string. You can hear the difference and actually see and adjust the resulting EQ curve.

Creating Textures with the Morph Pad

Another dramatic option in the modulation section is the Morph Pad, directly beneath the Material Pad, which allows you to adjust multiple parameters at once. In fact, all the parameters that are manipulated are indicated in orange. The path of the ball can be drawn in and stored as part of the patch. Just select the Record Trigger, hold down a note, and record your movement by dragging the red ball in the center. Release the trigger and listen to the new trajectory that your sound will follow every time you play it. You will easily achieve complex, cinematic sounds.

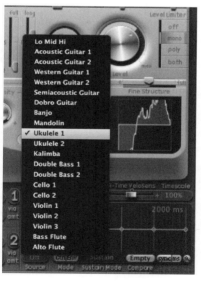

The EQ or Body of the instrument

The Morph Pad

EVOC 20's Retro Character

Vocoding 101

We all have heard the robot voice effect of a vocoder. Here's a summary of the technology behind it. A vocoder is an audio processor that captures the characteristic elements of an audio signal, and then uses this characteristic signal to affect other audio signals. Vocoding was initially used to synthesize speech. The basic component extracted during the vocoder analysis is called the *formant*. The formant describes the fundamental frequency of a sound and its associated noise components.

The classic vocoder works like this: the input signal (for example, my voice saying, "Hello, my name is Dot") is fed into the vocoder's input. This audio signal is sent through a series of filters that create a signature of the input signal, based on the frequency content. The signal to be processed (a synthesized string sound, for example) is fed into another input on the vocoder. The filter signature created above during the analysis of your voice is used to filter the synthesized sound. The audio output of the vocoder contains the synthesized sound modulated by the filter created by your voice. You hear a synthesized sound that pulses to the tempo of your voice input with the tonal characteristics of your voice added to it. Modulating even a synth or a string patch by a drumbeat or other rhythm track creates some very cool pulsing textures that reinforce the groove.

EVOC 20 PolySynth and EVOC 20 TrackOscillator

There are two vocoders in Logic, the EVOC 20 PolySynth (a software instrument) and the EVOC 20 TrackOscillator (an effects plug-in). Both use the same vocoding technology and have a similar interface and sonic quality. The main distinction is that EVOC 20 Polysynth has its own oscillators to generate sound and the EVOC 20 TrackOscillator is an effects plug-in that you place on an insert of another software instrument track. Let's start with the EVOC 20 TrackOscillator.

To Do:

- In an Empty Project, create a software instrument track and load an EXS24.
- Navigate in the Library to the Synthesizer folder, and then Synth Pads.
- Load the Basic Pad.
- Insert the EVOC 20 TrackOscillator on Insert 1 from the plug-ins folder (Filters > EVOC 20).
- Place an Apple Loop drumbeat on audio track 1.
- Select the Beats tag in the Apple Loops browser, and then try Analog Drum Machine 80.
- In the EVOC 20 Sidechain menu in upper right, select Track 1 from the menu.

EVOC 20 Sidechain Assignment to Track 1

- Play a 4-bar whole-note chord progression with the EXS24 pad, holding each chord for two bars.
- Start playback on the track to hear chords chopped and rhythmically playing the same rhythm as the drumbeat.
- Experiment with the EVOC 20 character by adjusting Formant Stretch, Formant Shift, and the Resonance knobs and the width of the blue bar above the Formant display.

Formant Stretch and Formant Shift

The Steps to the Classic Vocoder Vocal Effect

To Do:

- On a software instrument track, load the EVOC PS.
- On the sidechain in the upper right, place an audio track of a vocal.
- Select the EVOC PS preset Vintage Vocoder > Clear Voice Vocoder.
- With the EVOC PS instrument track selected, engage the transport in Play mode, and play a melody.

External MIDI, ReWire, and a Special Plug-In for Hardware Synths

You have two options with your external hardware synthesizers. The audio outputs of your hardware synthesizer naturally need to be cabled to your audio interface, and the MIDI ins and outs need to be cabled to a MIDI interface connected to the computer:

#1 External MIDI: Simply cable your keyboard to a MIDI interface recognized by the Audio MIDI Setup utility. Then, choose in Logic the External MIDI track from the Create Track menu. The Library will open on the right, and you can select your keyboard. This is also the procedure for any ReWire Instruments like Reason and Live.

#2 External Instrument: The External Instrument is a bit of a secret and a recent addition to the Logic feature set. It offers a more complete solution but requires another step. With the External Instrument, you can select the hardware synthesizer via this I/O insert on a software instrument channel strip in the same menu where you'd select the EXS24, Sculpture, ES2, and so on.

With the External Instrument, you can add Logic plug-in effects, either or an insert or via a send to an auxiliary channel strip, and even bounce the hardware parts to an audio track.

There are only two quick assignments to make in the External Instrument interface:

MIDI Destination: Choose the MIDI instrument (for example, Motif, Fantom, and so on) and MIDI channel 1–16.

Input field: Choose the inputs of your audio interface that the keyboard is cabled to.

There is a volume slider to adjust the incoming signal level, but this shouldn't need much adjustment after you've done your initial setup of the keyboard.

External Instrument for hardware synths

Chapter 11: "Good Housekeeping and Other Smart Practices" also covers the steps of adding the patch names to a multi-instrument in the Environment so the preset can be recalled from the hardware synth when you reload the Logic session. With the External Instrument steps described above, you will have to keep a log and manually scroll to the correct patch. What we have achieved for the moment is being able to easily trigger an external keyboard.

Power Tip: Project Template for Your Hardware Synths

The External Instrument provides easy access to any hardware synths cabled to your audio interface by specifying what input the instrument is cabled to on your audio interface and which MIDI channel you want to use. This information can be stored in a default song as a Custom Project template so that they're always ready to go when you start a new project.

Using Third-Party Software instruments

When you install a third-party software instrument, you may have to launch the Audio Units Manager and select Reset & Rescan Selection to ensure that it is recognized by Logic.

The third-party instruments will show up in the same menu on a channel strip as Logic instruments. They will appear in the lower half of the menu under the menu heading AU Instruments, which stands for Audio Unit Instruments and refers to the protocol for third-party plug-ins that Apple introduced with OS X.

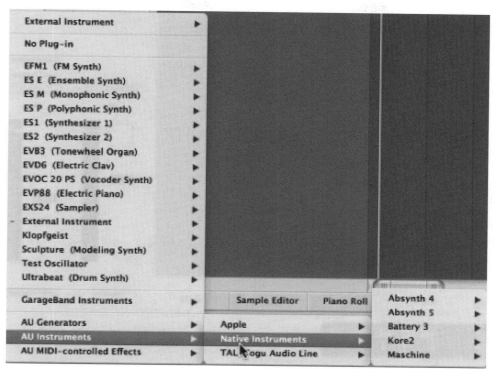

Third-party instruments in Logic

Unfortunately, third-party instrument presets will not automatically show up in the Library when you select the instrument. The only way to store your settings there is to include them in channel strip settings that will then be visible in the Library.

Controlling Synth Parameters from Knobs and Sliders

Making assignments to physical knobs and sliders is easy. From the Preferences menu in the Arrange toolbar, select Controller Assignments (Preferences > Controller Assignments). You can leave the default tab on Easy view.

Choose Preferences > Controller Assignments.

Hit the Learn mode button in the lower right of the window.

Touch the onscreen Logic parameter you want to control.

Turn the physical knob or slider on your hardware controller.

Be sure to turn the knob or slider a full rotation so that the controller assignment covers the full range of movement on the knob or slider. That's it! Now have some fun tweaking all the great Logic instruments.

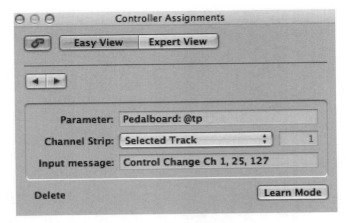

Controller assignments in Easy mode

Chapter 8

AMAZING THINGS TO DO WITH APPLE LOOPS

Apple Loops are your best friend in Logic, especially if you apply techniques for slicing, processing, and otherwise manipulating audio and MIDI in Logic. Apple Loops are audio or MIDI files (blue versus green, respectively), with metadata that allow them to lock in real time to the correct tempo and key when dragged into your project. While tempo sync is automatic, locking in pitch does require a quick assignment in the global tracks, explained below.

The Logic Studio provides tons of royalty-free factory Apple Loops in the Loop Browser, more than 20 gigabytes, including the entire collection of five Jam Packs that initially sold separately for $99 each. These Jam Pack Apple Loops—World, Orchestral, Remix, Rhythm Section, Vocal, and so on—offer not just audio loops but also instrument loops that load with the Logic instrument and settings. This allows you to do additional MIDI programming that can help the loop conform even tighter to your own style and feel.

Apple Loops have made an interesting entrance into the landscape of beat making. While many commercial songwriters and producers have embraced these license-free loops, there are still those producers who believe it's okay to sample a record but not use an Apple Loop. The perception is that somehow it is cheating, while samples are "legit." Everyone should choose the tools that inspire them and feel right for their workflow, but it is a bit ironic to see using license-free loops (Apple Loops) as cheating, but using uncleared samples from records a good idea. It's all part of the complicated and fascinating era of music we live in.

What Is an Apple Loop? (Blue Versus Green Loops)

An Apple Loop is a prerecorded drumbeat, rhythm part, melody line, or other musical pattern that can be repeated seamlessly. It contains metadata with descriptive keywords (tags) used by the Loop Browser to filter searches by instrument, genre, and mood. It differs from a regular audio file in that it follows Logic's project key and tempo. All of these Apple Loops are license-free, which means you do not need permission to use them in a commercial release.

There are two types of Apple Loops, which show up color-coded in the Loop Browser. There are the blue Apple Loops (audio only) and the green Apple Loops containing the original MIDI performance plus software instrument and effect settings. Their color is also indicated by the icon: green MIDI loops have the icon of a music note, and the blue audio loops have an icon of an audio waveform.

Name	▼	Tempo	Key	Beats	Match	Fav
80s Pop Beat 22		110		16	89%	☐
80s Pop Beat 23		110	–	8	90%	☐
80s Pop Beat 24		110	–	16	90%	☐
Classic Rock Beat 06		140	–	16	71%	☐
Classic Rock Beat 07		140	–	16	71%	☐
Classic Rock Beat 08		140	–	16	71%	☐
Classic Rock Beat 09		140	–	16	71%	☐
Classic Rock Beat 10		140	–	16	71%	☐
Effected Drum Kit 16		110	–	8	90%	☐
Effected Drum Kit 19		100	–	8	78%	☐
Effected Drum Kit 21		95	–	8	73%	☐
Effected Drum Kit 23		90	–	8	66%	☐
Effected Drum Kit 25		90	–	8	66%	☐
Effected Drum Kit 26		85	–	4	58%	☐

Blue versus green Apple Loops

Auditioning and Using Loops in Your Project

You can audition loops in real time while playing your song by simply selecting them. This allows you to experiment with beats and sounds before adding the loops to your arrangement. Click a second time to stop playback.

When you are ready to add a loop to your project, drag the loop into the Arrange window, and a new track will automatically be created. Or, drop the loop directly onto any empty audio track. To repeat a loop in your arrangement, drag the upper right corner to the desired length. When you hover over the sweet spot in the upper right of region, the Pointer tool turns into a semicircle-shaped tool, the Region Looping tool. Use the same tool to break and end the loop, even midway through a loop.

Reset ⊗	Acoustic	Bass	All Drums
Favorites	Electric	Guitars	Kits
All	Clean	Piano	Beats
Rock/Blues	Distorted	Elec Piano	Shaker
Electronic	Dry	Organ	Tambourine
World	Processed	Synths	Percussion
Urban	Grooving	Strings	Bell
Jazz	Cinematic	Horn	Timpani
Country	Relaxed	Woodwind	Cymbal
Melodic	Intense	Brass	Vinyl
Orchestral	Cheerful	Mallets	»

Name	▼	Tempo	Key	Beats	Match	Fav
80s Pop Beat 22		110		16	89%	☐
80s Pop Beat 23		110	–	8	90%	☐
80s Pop Beat 24		110	–	16	90%	☐
Classic Rock Beat 06		140	–	16	71%	☐
Classic Rock Beat 07		140	–	16	71%	☐
Classic Rock Beat 08		140	–	16	71%	☐
Classic Rock Beat 09		140	–	16	71%	☐
Classic Rock Beat 10		140	–	16	71%	☐
Effected Drum Kit 16		110	–	8	90%	☐
Effected Drum Kit 19		100	–	8	78%	☐
Effected Drum Kit 21		95	–	8	73%	☐
Effected Drum Kit 23		90	–	8	66%	☐
Effected Drum Kit 25		90	–	8	66%	☐
Effected Drum Kit 26		85	–	4	58%	☐

Auditioning Apple Loops in the Loop Browser

Repeating an Apple Loop in the Arrange window

Power Tip: The Loop Browser's Audio Playback Track

This is obscure information that will be relevant only in rare circumstances but could save you from scratching your head—and besides, you may just be curious. Apple Loops previewed in the Loop Browser play back through the last available audio track defined by your mixer (for example, Track 32, Track 64). The advantage of them not playing back through, say, audio track 1 means that this will generally avoid any confusion of the loop being previewed with plug-ins.

Musical Tags and the Search Engine

The musical tags in the Loop Browser allow you to narrow down your search by clicking on one or multiple descriptor tags (for example, Urban, Beats). When you are ready to start another search, hit the Reset tag in the upper left to reset the Browser. In the upper left of the View menu directly above the descriptor tags, you can narrow down your search to a particular Apple Loop library. The default is Show All, but you can search within one Jam Pack, for example. This can really speed up your navigation. The Tempo and Key columns in the Loop Browser table provide the original tempo and pitch of the Loop, which, of course, you're not limited to.

The other search option is to type a keyword into the search field if you have a specific loop in mind and know part of its name. A handy feature while you're shopping is the option to add to your Favorites by checking the Fav column on the far right. This way you can keep any loops for a project you may work on later in your Apple Loops "shopping cart."

Hit Songs Using Apple Loops

While many commercially released songs and soundtracks utilize Apple Loops, few became as viral an inside-industry joke as two R&B hit songs that prominently featured Apple Loops, with little manipulation or disguise:

Usher's "Love in This Club," produced by Polow da Don. Two Apple Loops are taken directly from the Jam Pack Remix Tools: Euro Hero Synth 02 and Euro Hero Synth 03. What's so bold about the production of this song (which topped the Billboard Hot 100 list) is that these Apple Loops unabashedly provide the main melodic hook.

Rihanna's "Umbrella," produced by Tricky Stewart and The Dream. The main drum track of the song is based on a standard Apple Loop found in GarageBand as well as

Bin	Loops	Library	Browser

View: Show All Signature: 4/4
Scale: Any (Q·)

Reset ⊗	Acoustic	Bass	All Drums
Favorites	Electric	Guitars	Kits
All	Clean	Piano	Beats
Rock/Blues	Distorted	Elec Piano	Shaker
Electronic	Dry	Organ	Tambourine
World	Processed	Synths	Percussion
Urban	Grooving	Strings	Bell
Jazz	Cinematic	Horn	Timpani
Country	Relaxed	Woodwind	Cymbal
Melodic	Intense	Brass	Vinyl
Orchestral	Cheerful	Mallets	»

Name ▼	Tempo	Key	Beats	Match	Fav
Beatbox Old School 08	80	-	2	50%	☐
Beatbox Old School 09	98	-	2	77%	☐
Beatbox Old School 10	96	-	4	75%	☐
Beatbox Old School 11	96	-	4	75%	☐
Beatbox Old School 12	94	-	4	72%	☐
Beatbox Old School 13	110	-	2	90%	☐
Beatbox Old School 14	82	-	4	53%	☐
Breaks DJ Dream Beat 01	128	-	8	87%	☐
Breaks DJ Dream Beat 02	128	-	8	87%	☐
Breaks DJ Dream Beat 03	128	-	8	87%	☐
Breaks DJ Dream Beat 04	128	-	8	87%	☐
Breaks DJ Dream Beat 05	128	-	8	87%	☐
Breaks DJ Dream Beat 06	128	-	8	87%	☐
Breaks DJ Dream Beat 07	128	-	8	87%	☐

Descriptor tags, the Reset tag, and the View menu

Logic: Vintage Funk Kit 03. This song earned Rihanna a Grammy with Jay-Z for Best Rap/Sung Collaboration and a nomination for Song of the Year.

Is this cheating? That is a philosophical conversation beyond the scope of this book, but if you have any misgivings as a producer, you may feel more comfortable by using them as a foundation that you layer with your own channel strip settings or perform any of the following creative edits to make them your own.

Tricks with Green Apple Loops

You have many easy ways to create your own variations with the green Apple Loops. If the green Apple Loop is a drum kit, you can easily separate out all the elements of the kit onto separate tracks from the local menu in the Arrange window (MIDI Menu > Separate MIDI Events > By Note Pitch), as explained in chapter 3 in the section "A Few Tricks to Help Your Creative Process." This is especially convenient if there is one clanging cowbell you want to delete from the loop, as in the next example.

Removing an Unwanted Element from a Drum Loop
- Drag Hip-hop Beat 12 from the Apple Loop library into the Arrange window.
- Select local MIDI Menu > Separate MIDI Events > By Note Pitch to separate the Apple Loop into eight regions on individual tracks.
- Highlight any region and enable Cycle by clicking into the shaded area in the upper half of the bar ruler.
- Select and preview each region one by one, using the "S" key to solo and hitting the Spacebar to play back.
- The fifth region from the top should be a pitched Triangle. Hit the "M" key to mute so that that region does not play back.
- Hit the "S" key again to take the project out of Solo mode and preview the modified Apple Loop, now minus the Triangle.
- To remove the Triangle permanently, make sure that that region is highlighted and then delete it with the Delete key.
- Select the remaining regions by lassoing around them with the Pointer tool.
- Hit the Escape key to access the floating toolbox, and choose the Glue tool.
- Click on any region with the Glue tool while all regions are selected to merge them back into one region of MIDI data.
- Tidy up the Arrange window by deleting the empty tracks created by Separate MIDI Events.
  Note: Keep this Logic project open for the next technique.

Changing the Software Instrument Playing Back the Loop

When you are shopping for an instrument riff in the Apple Loop library, keep in mind that any green Apple Loop may lay in the groove even better simply by changing the channel strip setting from its default to one that blends better with your production. Maybe it started as a Piano Apple Loop but will sound smoother in your groove with a different piano sound or even a clav, an electric piano, or any one of the synth channel strip settings. The possibilities are endless. Be sure to explore the warped folders with some very creative sound design of effects plug-in settings.

Take a minute now to experiment with changing the channel strip setting with the example below or with any green Apple Loop. Note: If you drag into the empty space in the Arrange area, it will automatically create a software instrument track, even though a green Apple Loop would play back on an Audio track. Click on the I/O insert that loaded in the leftmost channel strip in the Arrange window for the given track or the pane on top of the channel strip. Then start shopping in the Library for a preset or channel strip setting you like!

Use the Logic project above with Hip-hop Beat 12.

- In the Apple Loops browser, select the tabs Urban, Piano.
- Highlight Hip-hop Piano 01 to preview.
- Drag Hip-hop Piano 01 into the Arrange workspace, and a software instrument track will be created with the Grand Piano channel strip.
- Switch the Tab on the right from Loops to Library.
- With the piano track still highlighted, switch to the Keyboards folder in the Library. Select Warped Electric Piano > Late '60s Suitcase.
- Adjust the gain on the channel strip on the left so that the electric piano lays in the drum groove.

Changing the Quantize and Swing

Because green Apple Loops are essentially MIDI files, an obvious quick embellishment to their groove is to experiment with the Quantize and Swing in the Region Parameter box. This is a great technique if you drag in multiple drum Apple Loops and want to tighten the groove. Alternately, if the green Apple Loop is a pitched instrument, whether a piano or a string section, experiment with the Transpose in the Region Parameter box.

What you will learn in the next chapter is how to easily quantize audio with Flex Audio, which means that you'll be able to grab a handful of blue Apple Loop drumbeats (audio loops) and lock them tightly into a unique groove by setting them to the same quantize setting. Something to look forward to in chapter 9!

Making Your Own Apple Loops

You can quickly create your own Apple Loops, green or blue, right within Logic from the Region menu > Add to Apple Loops Library. This menu is applicable whether from a MIDI performance you programmed or an audio beat you brought into Logic.

All Apple Loops you add to Logic's library are saved here:
<home folder>/Library/Audio/Apple Loops/User Loops

The Add Region to Apple Loops Library dialog box requires that you make at least one selection of a relevant Instrument Descriptor tag on the left, and as many other Descriptor tags (for example, Acoustic, Distorted, and so on) on the right as appropriate. Your Apple Loops should contain the musical idea or riff from a single instrument that falls into one of the categories or musical tags in the Apple Loop browser.

To find your loop in the Apple Loop browser, select the keywords that match its description; it should then appear in the list below the table of Descriptor tags.

The quality of your Apple Loops can be improved by opening them in the Apple Loops Utility. The utility is located in the Applications/Utilities folder. Drag an entire folder of Apple Loops into the Apple Loops Utility to edit all at once.

Here, you can use the transient editor to improve the Apple Loop's sound quality. You can minimize artifacts by adjusting the

Add region to Apple Loops library

placement and number of transient markers. Experiment with tempo to make sure that the Apple Loop retains its sound quality, and add or subtract markers as needed.

Power Tip: Labeling Your Custom Apple Loops

A popular request of Logic users has been to be able to create their own descriptor tags and replace the factory ones in the Loop Browser if, for example, you know you'll never need the factory categories of Cheerful or Arrythmic loops. Unfortunately, there are valid reasons why it is not an option to create customized tags as far as compatibility with third-party loop libraries. A workaround when creating and labeling your own loops so you can locate them is to put your initials in front of every loop name as the first characters (for example, DBEdgySynth1), so you can at least search for your loops more easily in the Loop Browser's search field.

Indexing Your Loops in the Browser

Locate any loops you created or dragged in from a third-party DVD library in the Finder view, then drag the folder over the Apple Loop browser. A progress bar will indicate that the Loops are being added and indexed. It can feel a bit like you're not doing it right, but that's all there is to it.

Third-Party Apple Loop Libraries

The Apple Loop format has become enough of an industry standard that many third-party manufacturers of sample libraries now develop in the Apple Loop format as well. To install one of these libraries, it may simply be a folder of Apple Loops that you are directed to drag to your hard drive. After adding to your Loop library, index them as above from the Finder. These Loops will appear in the View menu at the bottom of the list, beneath the Jam Pack libraries.

Setting the Key (Changing Pitch)

To change the pitch of a green Apple Loop in the Arrange window, click-and-hold the transposition setting in the Region Parameter box in the Inspector, and drag up or down. The Apple Loops conform to the key of your Logic project. If you don't set a key in the Signature Track, Logic defaults to the key of C, which may not be the real key of the song.

Keep in mind, while you are auditioning Loops, you may direct Logic to preview in the Song Key by manually selecting it in the menu at the bottom right of the Loop Browser, labeled "Play in". This is affecting the loop's pitch only while it's being previewed. Once you drag it into the Arrange window, it will conform to the key set in the Signature Track.

	70s Electric Piano 03	90	C	8	91%	
	70s Electric Piano 04	90	C	8	91%	
	70s Electric Piano 05	90	C	16	91%	

495 items   Play in: Song Key

Play in Song Key menu

To adjust the Music Key globally for your Logic project, open up the Signature track in the global tracks. If the Signature track is not in view, click-and-hold on any track in the global tracks to find and enable view of the Signature track.

Double-click on the default key signature "C" (visible on the Signature track in the Arrange window workspace) to type in a new key for the project.

Changing key in the Signature track

Chapter 9
REMIXING AND MAKING BEATS

This chapter is the fun one if you're looking for production tricks. The first eight chapters got you driving, and now it's time to kick back in fifth gear with the creative power of Logic. Take your music in new directions with any of these techniques that catch your eye. They're all easy when you know how.

Grasping the depth of the new Flex Audio, Logic's elastic audio, should be at the heart of any remix work you do going forward in Logic. It's a lot to take in but worth every minute you spend exploring the suite of Flex tools.

This chapter also introduces a few special guests and friends: Jay-Z's engineer, Young Guru, and Mat Mitchell, who has shared his technical and creative genius in Logic with the likes of Nine Inch Nails, Tool, and Katy Perry.

It's All About Timing (and Stretching)

BPM Plug-in and Tap Tempo to Find Tempo

Locking audio files to the project tempo is key to any remixing work. There are many different techniques to achieve this in Logic, depending on the situation. The BPM plug-in is great for getting a quick readout of the tempo of a long audio file (for example, a song someone sent you or that you dragged in from iTunes).

The BPM plug-in is located in the Metering subfolder of Logic plug-ins. Just insert it on the audio track, start playback, and then give it a few seconds to read the file's tempo. You'll be surprised at how accurate it is when you switch Logic's tempo to the beats per minute that the plug-in finds and turn on the click in the transport.

Tap Tempo is a common technique used in computer-based music software and some drum machines to be able to manually tap out a tempo and have the sequencer clock update to that tempo. Tap Tempo in Logic has a few "gotcha's" to be aware of. For example, the transport must be stopped to tap in the tempo. This means that the audio file has to be playing on another machine or in another app like iTunes! Let's take a look at how it works, since it's such a popular question.

BPM Plug-In to Find Tempo

Here is the setup for how to use Tap Tempo in Logic:

- Choose File > Project Settings > Synchronization > Turn Sync mode to Manual.
- Be sure that the checkbox beneath Sync mode is checked "Auto enable external sync".
- The bar ruler will turn blue.
- Select a software instrument, and then tap at least four times with the Tap Tempo key command (the default is Shift + T).
- With Auto Sync enabled, Logic will jump into Manual sync mode after tapping the Tap Tempo key command four times.
- Logic's tempo in the transport will update accordingly.

Adjusting Logic's Tempo to the Beat (or the Vocal)

Here's the scenario: You have an audio sample of a beat, and you want to conform Logic's tempo to that sample. Sometimes you find a beat and realize what you started will actually sound better at the new tempo of the imported audio.

- First make sure that the sample is perfectly looping (whether 2, 4, 8 bars, and so on) and placed on a downbeat in Logic. To do this, highlight the audio file in the Arrange area, select the Set Locators tool in the toolbar and start playback.
- Logic will cycle the highlighted region. When it comes back around to the downbeat, listen for any hiccups in the beat (for example, hearing two kicks flamming or the downbeat kick dropping too soon).
- If necessary, create a perfect audio loop in the Arrange window with the zoom tools and Marquee tool for cutting (see chapter 5 for details). There is no need to go into the Sample Editor. If you are starting with a long audio file (for example, a whole record), use the Marquee tool to make loose cuts to bring the file size down closer to the target length of the loop, whether two or four bars.
- Zoom into the audio file while the audio is looping, with the Set Locators tool enabled in the toolbar and the region highlighted.
- Once the audio sample is perfectly looping, set the bar ruler cycle length to that same number of bars as the loop, whether 1, 2, 4, 8, and so on. The bar ruler will not match region length. For example, if it's a 4-bar loop, highlight four bars in Logic's bar ruler.
- From the Options menu, go to Tempo > Adjust Tempo Using Region Length and Locators.
- Logic's tempo will update to conform to the tempo of the audio loop. Easy!

Setting Logic's tempo to a sampled loop

You now changed Logic's tempo to conform to the tempo of the audio file! All you had to do is let Logic know how many bars the drum loop should equal in Logic.

Time-Stretching Audio to Logic's Tempo

More often the goal is the reverse—to lock an audio file or sampled loop to Logic's tempo. The audio source may be from a record or a sample library, or it may be one you recorded in your own studio. It's a common production technique to modify the loop's original tempo. This changes the tempo of the audio file and its length, but not its pitch. Once again, it starts with a trimmed audio file that is perfectly looping that you want to conform to Logic's tempo.

Below are the steps once it's a perfect loop.

- Highlight the region.
- In the bar ruler, select however many bars match the number of bars of the loop. If it is a 2-bar loop, select two bars in bar ruler.
- In the local audio menu, select Time Stretch Region to Locators.

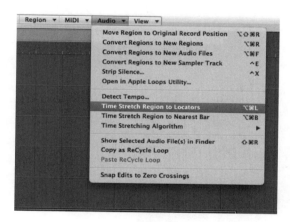

Time-stretching the loop to Logic's tempo

In this same local audio menu, you will find different time-stretching algorithms to experiment with. The default, Universal, is a good place to start. The Legacy Algorithms may prove useful for different types of material, such as Monophonic or Pads, for the situations that the names imply.

Below are the steps to adjust the tempo of a loop.

- Cycle the region and preview with a metronome to establish that the loop is not in time with the Logic tempo.
- Be sure to line up the Loop's downbeat with the downbeat of a bar in Logic (for example, Bar 1, Beat 1, or another bar on Beat 1).
- If your loop is slower than the project tempo, you will see that it extends beyond two bars in the bar ruler, if the loop itself is a two-bar loop. It needs to be sped up.
- Highlight the loop, and then manually select two bars in the bar ruler.
- Select local audio menu in Arrange > Time Stretch Region to Locators.
- Watch as the imported audio loop "shrinks" to perfectly fit the two-bar length selected in the bar ruler.

Option-Drag to Time-Stretch Audio

Logic also now allows you to time-stretch or compress an audio region directly in the Arrange area, without changing its pitch. This is the same technique that has been available for years for MIDI data. Simply Option-drag the end point of the region to where you want it to end, and the speed of the beat will be adjusted.

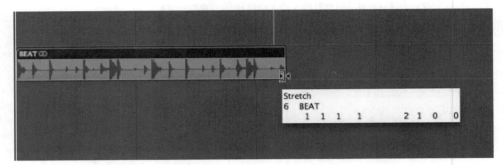

Option-Drag to time-compress or time-stretch

Power Tip: Time-Stretching with Snap to Absolute Value

Time-stretching with the Option-drag technique works especially well with the new Snap to Absolute Value option in the Snap menu in the upper right of the Arrange window. Snapping to absolute value constrains your edits to the nearest defined snap point as defined in this menu (for example, Beat, Bar, and so on).

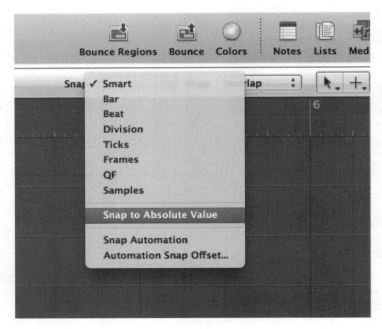

Snap to Absolute Value

Importing and Exporting Vocals for Remixing

The Track Import and Export menus are designed quite well in Logic. Be sure to explore all their submenus, and you will find a wide variety of import and export scenarios addressed.

Track Import

Let's start with Track Import. If someone sends you a vocal stem, you can simply drag it into the Logic Arrange area and can try the BPM plug-in if that information was not provided.

If it's a vocal or other musical element from another Logic project on your drive or a connected drive, there is a very thorough procedure available.

- Go to the Media section on the right.
- Choose the Browser tab.
- Click on the small pull-down menu defaulting to "Logic" next to left/right arrows and small icons to access your Finder from within Logic.
- Navigate to your Logic project on hard drive or any connected drives.
- Select the Logic song-file name—not the project folder.
- Choose the Import button in bottom right of the Browser area.
- All tracks of the Logic project will be in view in a Table format. Select the vocal or other audio files to import.
- Enable the Global tab to import the Tempo track of the audio file if desired. Easy!

Track Export

If you are providing audio stems to someone else performing a remix or maybe creating a remix of your own material, Logic has great options for exporting audio.

- From the File menu in the Arrange window, select the Export menu.
- Choose Export Track As Audio File or All Tracks As Audio Files.

This will create a complete audio stem or stems beginning at the top of the song and continuing until the end. Any separate regions on the track(s) will be combined into new continuous audio file(s). Access the same Export menu by Ctrl-clicking or right-clicking directly on the audio file.

Flex Audio ("Elastic Audio")

Flex Audio is Logic's interpretation of "elastic audio," which make it painless to adjust the timing, tempo, and rhythm of your audio tracks. After enabling Flex view in the toolbar and selecting an algorithm to analyze the transients on an audio track, you are able to make infinite changes to the timing of a beat or the phrasing and musical inflection of a vocal track.

Enabling Flex Mode

Enabling Flex mode in the toolbar opens up this universe of elastic time. Once enabled, you'll find a menu of modes to choose from inside the track header on the track list for each audio track. In that menu you can choose which Flex mode or algorithm is appropriate for the task at hand. For beats, it's generally best to use Slicing or Rhythmic.

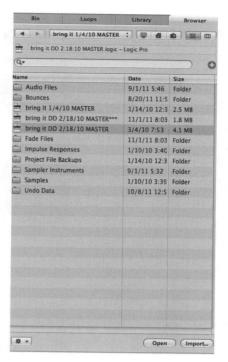

The Track Import menu

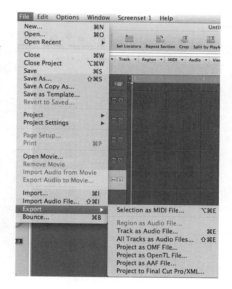

The Track Export menu

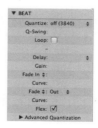

Enabling Flex per region

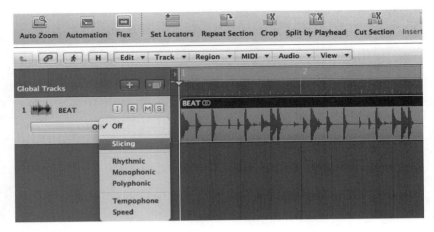

Selecting Flex mode on a track

Once you select a mode, the transients are detected on that track and visible as thin white lines in the waveform. And then you have access to infinite remix possibilities. Since Flex editing is completely nondestructive, you can enable and disable it for an individual region at any time in the Region Parameter box.

Flex Markers

The flex markers are the vertical lines with little orange handles at the top. These are the edit points that can be dragged forward and backward in time to expand or compress the audio that came before and change your musical phrasing. Specifically, flex markers determine the boundaries of your flex edits. The visual feedback in Flex view is fantastic. Color coding helps you see at a glance what portions of the audio are getting affected and how. Green indicates time compression, and red reveals time expansion.

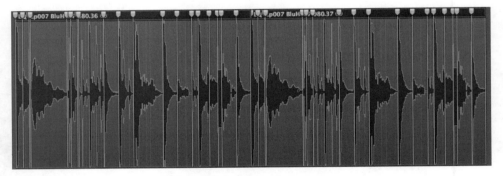

Flex markers, color coding of Flex Time compression and expansion

To add a new flex marker, click in the upper half of the waveform and a flex marker will be created at the clicked position. Moving a flex marker to the left time-compresses the preceding audio material, and moving it to the right time-expands the preceding audio material from any preceding flex marker up to the moved flex marker. Flex markers can be dragged either by the heavy white line over the waveform or by the orange handle above. Do not confuse the heavy white line of the flex marker with the thin, faint white lines that represent transients! To delete a flex marker, simply double-click on it.

Quantizing and Regrooving Your Audio

Once transients are detected on a track, the same Quantize menu in the Region Parameter box is available to audio as with MIDI. Simply select the Quantize value and Swing percentage as you would for a MIDI file, and experiment with the groove. If the transients have not been detected, the Quantize parameter is not available to an audio file in the Region Parameter box. Only a hyphen ("-") will be visible instead of the quantize parameter.

Flex Trick #1: Cutting on Transients

One of my favorite remix tricks is the Slice At Transient Markers, accessed by Ctrl-clicking on the region header in the Arrange workspace. (Note: The Region header is the thin area at the top of the region where the track name is located that turns black when the region is highlighted.) This can be performed without even enabling Flex mode on the track. Once you've sliced on the transients, there are an infinite number of creative possibilities. You can easily mute or cut between transients to create breakdowns in the groove.

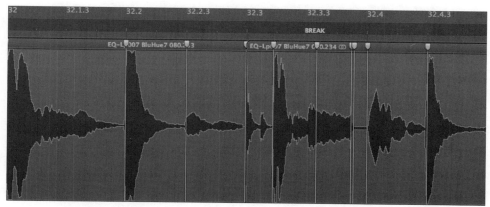

Flex markers versus transients

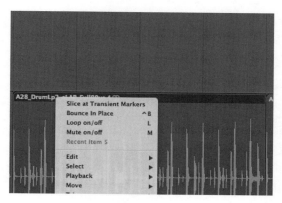

Slice at transient markers

Flex Trick #2: Special Effects with Tempophone

The Tempophone algorithm in Flex mode borrows from the analog world, introducing pitched, mechanical-sounding artifacts into the beat when you stretch the audio by dragging apart the transients. The algorithm emulates an actual device called a *tempophone*, which was originally developed in Germany and used years ago with magnetic tape to allow an engineer to vary the tempo and pitch of audio independently with a particular character. Generally, those two variables of tempo and pitch are interdependent when manipulated in the analog world. This machine was used to create new timbral characteristics by moving the tape across multiple tape playheads on a cylinder in varying direction and speed. Consider it a special effect for the right creative situation.

Tempophone Flex Mode

Power Tool: Flexing to Change Your Project Tempo

Ready for the ultimate remix tool using Flex Audio? You can change the tempo of your project by flexing it. First, enable Flex mode in the toolbar, and then choose a mode to detect transients on all your tracks. Now, you can change the tempo in the Logic transport, and all the tracks will conform to the new tempo.

Note: You can group-select all tracks and then select an algorithm on any one of the tracks' track header. The transients will be detected for your entire project at once to prepare for an efficient global tempo adjustment in the transport.

To create a track group in Logic, click-hold in the gray-shaded pane on a track's channel strip just above the fader and panner, and the Group pull-down menu is revealed. Here you can create a new group, name it, and select which parameters are active. The grouping pane on each channel strip reveals the group assignment at a glance.

Making Beats with Live Drummers

For the growing number of bands recording themselves in Logic, there are great production tools available for the band members or the mix engineer to fatten up or replace the sounds afterward.

Beat Mapping

While you can always edit in Logic against a time ruler with the bar ruler, there are situations when it's better to have the bar and beat grid conformed to the audio. If you're working with audio that was recorded free-form and without a click track, you may want to maintain this original human feel. You can create a tempo map of the multiple tempos if the live musicians didn't play at a consistent tempo (whether intentionally or not). This is easily achieved with Logic's Beat Mapping track found in the global tracks.

- Open the view by clicking on the disclosure triangle to the left of the name Global Tracks at the top of the track list.
- If Beat Mapping track is not in view, Ctrl-click and enable the Beat Mapping global track.
- Select the Kick track performed by the live drummer. Move this track adjacent to the global track to see what you're doing more easily.
- With the Kick track highlighted, select Detect in the Beat Mapping track to detect tempo.
- The transients identified for the Kick will be visible as white vertical lines displayed in the

lower half of the Beat Mapping track.

- The top half of the Beat Mapping track displays the bar ruler grid. Zoom in tightly to perform the next step.
- Listen to the Kick and drag the downbeat of a bar marking to the actual transient. A resulting tempo will be created, with fractions of a beat up to four decimal points. Check your work by creating even two-bar cycles anywhere.

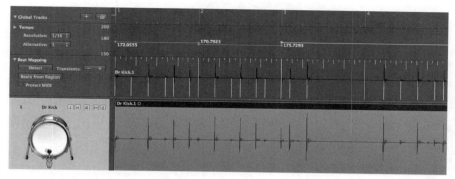

Beat-mapping by transient in global tracks

Drum Replacement

Drum Replacement is a great example of a production tool in Logic Studio that helps musicians achieve professionally engineered results on their own. Logic's Drum Replacement takes a technique used for years by experienced audio engineers and simplifies the process down to a few steps.

For example, imagine you didn't get the best sonic recording of a drummer's kick, although you really like the part the drummer played. Drum Replacement fixes this up pretty fast.

- Highlight the Kick audio track in the Arrange window.
- Select Drum Replacement from the local track menu (Track > Drum Replacement/ Doubling).
- Under the menu, you can choose Replacement or Doubling, Threshold, and so on. For now choose Replacement, and the live Kick recording will be muted.
- Logic will create an EXS24 Sampler Instrument folder beneath, detect the drum hits, and create a MIDI performance on the EXS track.
- The Library opens to a folder of Single Drums to replace (or double) the Kick.
- If desired, in Library select a different type of Single Drum that you want to replace (for example: Kick or Snare). The Library updates to bring your choice into view.

The Threshold determines how sensitive Logic should be when determining which hits in the audio file it should create note triggers for. The setting will depend on the relative level of the recorded drum and how well it is isolated from other signal sources and not experiencing bleed from other instruments.

The technique was available for years in Logic as the Audio To Score feature in the Sample Editor (Factory > Audio To Score) and was used with great success by many professional Logic users to create MIDI notes from a selected audio file.

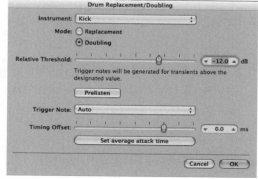

Drum Replacement with EXS24 in the Track menu

Let's hear what engineer Mat Mitchell has to say about Logic's Audio To Score:

Timing is the main thing I am looking for when I use Audio To Score, and the timing accuracy is great. The harmonic aspect requires a bit more tweaking by hand, but the results are worth it. If I'm working with drums, I'll just use a Transform function to pull all the note data to the correct spot.

I start with the preset just to get things in the ballpark. Second, I'll adjust the Velocity Threshold and Granulation until the "Result" indicators match the audio transients.

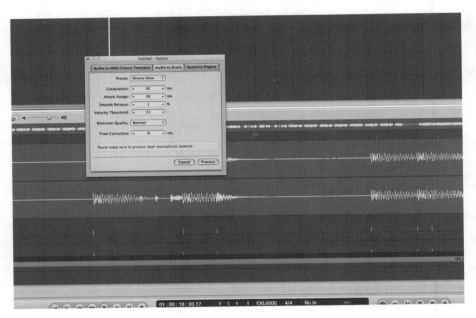

Mat Mitchell's Audio To Score

What Varispeed Is for Anyway

Varispeed is great for quickly trying out your whole session at another tempo or for slowing it down to rehearse before a live performance of a difficult passage. You can adjust between the range of 50% and 200% of the original tempo.

You can't bounce a project while in Varispeed mode, and you really don't want to work for hours with it enabled because it's taxing on the CPU. That said, it's a great tool if you need to rehearse a part at a slower tempo or quickly experiment with another tempo. If you decide that you prefer the new tempo, making the permanent tempo change to all your tracks should be performed with Flex Audio, as explained above.

Below are the steps to use Varispeed:

- Click-and-hold into the empty space of the Transport bar area so the Customize dialog opens so that the sheet of Transport menu is in view.
- Enable the Varispeed checkbox.
- Varispeed values will now display in the middle of the transport.
- Click on the word "Varispeed" in the transport to change how Varispeed is viewed. Switch to show Resulting Tempo, and then double-click into that field to enter the desired tempo.

- The Transport area will turn bright orange and the Logic tempo temporarily updates.
- You will also see the Varispeed transport button on the right, with a plus and minus symbol to enable and disable the Varispeed function.

Varispeed view in transport

How Logic Swings: Groove Templates

This is as classic a tool in Logic, as it gets and at the core of why early die-hard Logic users became such strong evangelists.

Logic allows you to highlight any audio or MIDI data and create a template for quantizing other tracks, called a "groove template." These can also be imported from your favorite drum machines and then fine-tuned with Logic's collection of quantize and swing parameters in the Region Parameter box. To create a groove template, simply highlight the MIDI file, and then select Make Groove Template at the bottom of the quantize menu (Quantize > Make Groove Template) in the Region Parameter box.

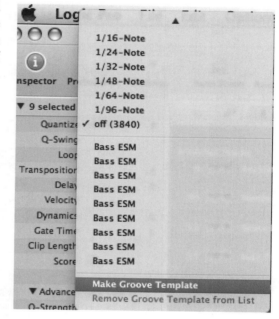

Making a groove template

These templates live as MIDI files within a song—there is no physical location on your hard drive where you can point to the folder of groove templates. What you can do is save the song containing the groove templates as your default song. In the "old days," this was referred to as your Logic Autoload—today it is called your Empty Project template.

Jay-Z's longtime engineer Young Guru has sworn by the swing in Logic for years because of the groove templates. He learned how to make groove templates by reading the manual, of all things! Below you'll find, in his own words, how he brought the grooves of the MPC into Logic by hand, not downloading those passed around on the Internet. Beyond this specific and powerful feature he shares, take note of the larger message of how Guru became "One with Logic" himself—by jumping in and starting to use Logic, and reading the manual:

I found out about groove templates by reading the manual. Like everyone else I just started using Logic, then eventually I started reading the manual to find out everything I could. What was exciting to me was that Logic really solved the problem of why I would stay in a beat machine like the MPC until then. The groove templates allowed me to bring the swing of that beat machine into Logic. I started to see the Logic groove templates on the Internet, but I didn't want to trust those so I followed the instructions in the manual of how to make your own. I thought it was unique to make your own out of audio, for example out of "Impeach the President." Then I could replace the groove with the drums from another breakbeat.

It's very easy in Logic with the combination of the groove template and Audio To MIDI to create MIDI notes from audio, and then put the swing back on yourself. Once I have it in Logic, I adjust certain things. If I love the swing, I can affect that swing further like with the Delay, something small that locks the drums into whatever music is going on. You'll have a sample of someone playing the instrument live. It may be off by a couple of milliseconds because of the natural performance. You like the overall swing but you just wish he'd lay back a little bit. If I was in the studio with the drummer, that's what I'd say to him.

You have the ability to import your MPC sequences into Logic. The internal MPC format of the .seq files appear as MIDI tracks in Logic. When I was transferring sessions into Logic, I'd pull up Battery that reads the MPC patch then I'd import the sequence. I'd save all my MPC 3000 files to a Zip drive, make a folder on my computer of MPC with audio and sequences, import the sequences then add the swing that perfectly emulates the MPC. If I had the groove at 53% in the MPC, now I can further adjust my music, maybe try one of Logic's templates, maybe that sounds better.

When you import the sequence from the MPC, Track 1 is the Kick. It's all labeled with all the original names when I click to import it. It's very clever the way it does it. Logic imports each track from my MPC with the same labels used in the MPC, like Kick, Snare, HH, Bass, and Strings.

I keep groove templates from the MPC and SP1200 in my Logic Autoload (Project template). I have 26 for the MPC and 12 for SP1200. "50, 51, 52…" are the swings for the 16th note in the SP1200. There's a swing feature in the MPC when you go to Sequence Edit. 50% is the normal swing so 51% is a percentage of the swing.

It's all about me trying to lock into whatever is going on musically with the drum programming. If I want it to be a little sloppier or a little tighter, I get into the Q-strength and Delay in Logic. I don't go down past 90% on the Q-strength. It starts at 100 and I don't have to go past 90%. It's like physically telling a drummer to play a little sloppier or a little behind the beat, but I love what you're doing—you're almost right there.
—*Young Guru*

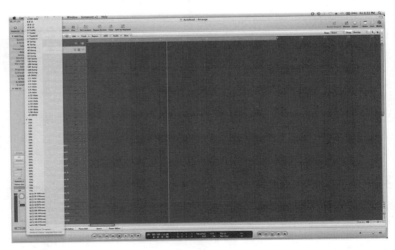

Young Guru's groove templates from the MPC and SP1200

▼ 6 selected	
Quantize:	1/4–Note ⇕
Q-Swing:	+74%
Loop:	☐
Transposition:	⇕
Delay:	⇕
Velocity:	*
Dynamics:	⇕
Gate Time:	⇕

Q-Swing!

Advanced Quantizing: Deepening the Groove

The Region Parameter box is one of the most powerful collections of tools for modifying MIDI on earth. Q-Swing in the Region Parameter box alters the position of every second point in the quantize grid. The grid is based on the start of the region. So if the region does not start on the downbeat, Q-Swing will affect the first and third notes. Drag the start of the region to a downbeat to fix it.

You should also explore the lower half of the Region Parameter box as Young Guru references above. There is a set of quantize parameters that are not visible unless the disclosure triangle is enabled. They are the secret of subtle fine-tuning of your groove. Explore Q-Strength, Q-Range, Q Flam, and so on, by setting their levels to the extreme and seeing if the groove lays further in the pocket.

DJ and Electronic Music Tricks

Here are a few quick and easy techniques that will especially appeal to producers of electronic music or any musicians wanting to introduce a modern element to their projects.

Space Designer Warping

This is such a quick and easy way to build a pulsing groove that it feels like cheating. In the folder of Space Designer presets is a folder called Warped Effects, which has quite a few subfolders of warped impulse responses. One of the most instantly powerful is the one at the top labeled Drone Tones. Try any drum loop through these presets, and you are sure to transform the beat in extremely musical ways for building a groove.

The normal usage of a convolution reverb like Space Designer is to make an impulse response (IR) of a room. Here, however, the IRs aren't reverb samples, but rather they are synth tones—actually AIFF files that you can view and listen to from the Finder: Library/Audio/Impulse Responses/Apple/05 Warped/01 Drone Tones

Or, in the IR drop-down window, there is a Show in Finder option.

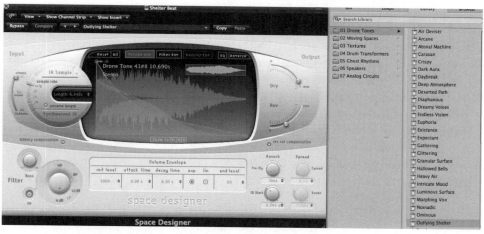

Space Designer Warped Effects presets

On the accompanying DVD-ROM is an example of one drum groove transformed a number of times with different Warped Effects Space Designer presets, building the entire foundation of the groove. Have a listen and then experiment yourself with processing your own drumbeat with Space Designer Warped Effects presets.

DJ Speed Fades

This is very slick and couldn't be easier. Speed Fades introduce a ramp up or down in tempo, within an audio region and the *shwooshing* artifacts of turntable tricks to accent the buildup of a section of your arrangement. They are drawn onto the corner of an audio region like traditional fades.

To select a Speed Fade, highlight the target region in the Arrange window, then select from the menu in the Region Parameter box under Fade In To Speed Up or under Fade Out To Speed Down. Directly next to the type of fade you select, you can adjust the numeric value for the amount. As you increase the value, you will see a more dramatic slope to the fade visible in orange on the audio file, and then adjust the fade curve with the parameter beneath. Experiment with extreme values!

Try this: Separate the last bar of one of the Effected Drum Kit 8 or 16-bar Apple Loops with the Marquee tool. Add a one-half-bar-long "slow down" speed fade, and then adjust Curve in the Region Parameter box to find the perfect curve for your speed fade.

Speed Fades

Making a Sampler Instrument Out of a Drum Loop

There is now a tool for creating an EXS24 Sampler Instrument in literally one move. However, if you do it in only one step, you may not be entirely happy with your results. It's still quick, but there are a few fine-print adjustments that will improve your results. Let's start by taking a look at that one move.

- Highlight an audio region; start with any drum loop (though you could certainly use other instruments).
- Select from the local audio menu in the Arrange, Convert Regions To New Sampler Tracks. An EXS24 instrument and MIDI region is automatically created on the track beneath.

The problem with this feature is that Logic is taking all the detected transients and turning them into EXS24 zones. That means that if there is a teeny tiny noise in the audio file, it may get assigned to a zone, and thus a key, in your drum kit. Or, if two of the same kicks are hit in a row in the drum loop, they will each become a zone and you'll have the same drum sound assigned to two consecutive notes on your keyboard.

Here's what you do to create a useful EXS24 Sampler Instrument with this feature.

- Before you select Convert Regions in the audio menu, open up the Sample Editor view of your source audio file.
- Select Audio File > Detect Transients.
- Here you can clean up which transients are being detected.
- To preview between two transients, highlight and then click on the speaker in the local menu. Or change the Alternate tool in the Sample Editor to Solo, then highlight between two transients while pressing the Command key.
- To remove a detected transient, double-click directly on it.
- Drag to change its location or use the Pencil tool to introduce a transient.

- After you're satisfied with the cleanup, go back to the Arrange window and local audio menu to create the EXS24 instrument and you should be quite satisfied with the results.

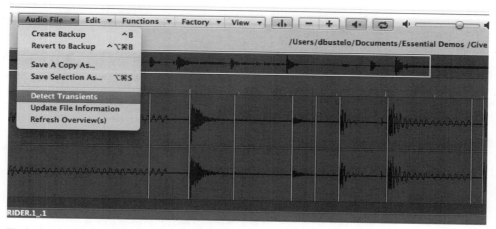

Playing between transients selection in Sample Editor

Retro Logic Groove Tricks

This section of the book is at the heart of the appeal of Logic in its earliest years. You will find that these tools stand the test of time as far as facilitating the creation of fresh beats in any musical genre.

Transform Editor for "Human" Drummer Feels and Fills

The Transform Editor is as old-school Logic as it gets and is the reason that Logic users like Mat Mitchell are so excited to be Logic users. Don't be fooled by its interface, which looks a bit dry and geeky. There is so much you can do here to humanize the feel of your music and solve problems; once you focus your eye, it's very easy to use. You will be the master of your MIDI performances and will have the power to make them all feel as human as you want.

From the Arrange window, select Window > Transform. Then, from the list of presets in the upper left of the window, select Humanize. We'll use this preset to take the tour.

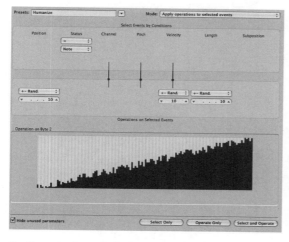

The Humanize Preset in the Transform Editor

The Transform window has two main sections, indicated by large shaded rectangles in a stack. The one on top is labeled as Select Events By Condition. The area beneath is labeled Operations On Selected Events. The top shaded Select Events rectangle is where you choose what type of events you want to affect. In this Humanize preset, only Note events will be affected, as indicated by the event selected under the heading labeled Status.

In the rectangle below, three types of operations are selected to be performed, randomizing the Note Position, Velocity, and Length. If you think about it, these are scientific equivalents of the "human" elements that any good musician uses to create a "feel" within his or her performance.

The diagram beneath is your visual feedback to the operation, and at the very bottom of the screen in the lower right is where you can select the operation, listen back, and then select it again until you are satisfied with the randomization.

Experiment with all the presets or create your own Transform setting at the bottom of the list using, Create Initialized User Set. When you launch, you see all possible types of events on the top row and all types of operations possible beneath. Choose what operations you want to do, then you can select in the lower left the checkbox to Hide Unused Parameters. This way you can clean up the view and focus on only the operations you plan to use, not all possible operations.

Here's what Mat Mitchell says about the Transform window, which he named one of the four most creative tools in Logic:

> Transform is great as a quick way to modify MIDI data. Four presets I use a lot are
> 1. Scale: I use this if I need to limit the dynamic range of a performance.
> 2. Double Speed/Half Speed Presets: Quick and easy presets.
> 3. Fixed Note Length: I use this quite a bit if I have played in a part and want to have a tight quantized sound. It's a quick way to match all note lengths.
> 4. Fixed Pitch: I use this quite a bit with Audio To Score on drums to pull notes to the correct pitch quickly.

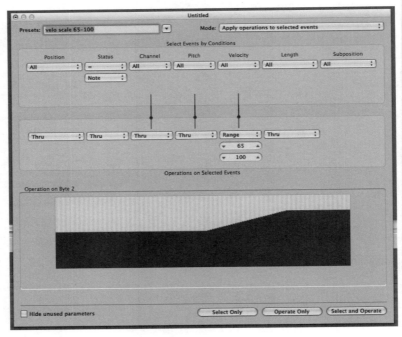

Mat Mitchell's Transform window presets

The Transform window is also your best solution to even out and, in effect, fix the velocities of a keyboard performance of, say, a synth bassline played from a keyboard. The first preset in the list, Fixed Velocity, solves the above problem.

Gate Time and Delay

This is as old-school Logic as you can get when it comes to getting creative and more "human" with your groove in Logic. The early years of computer-based sequencing were cursed with the association of making music that sounded robotic. Logic was a pioneer in proving this assumption as wrong, with features in the Region Parameter box that are still favorite tricks of diehard Logic users like Mat Mitchell, whose work for A Perfect Circle, Nine Inch Nails, Tool, Puscifer, and Katy Perry, can be found on countless records and live shows, proving that technique transcends musical genre. When you learn it well, you can create in any style of music, and you will be asked to!

Mat's humble explanation for how he became so advanced with Logic is simply that he has been using it every day since Logic 3 came out. The implied advice for becoming "One with Logic" is once again to just keep using it. Every day.

That said, the Gate Time and Delay are two of Mat's favorite tools. In his own words:

> Select a region or track. In the Region Parameters box on the upper left you can adjust Delay. I use this for technical things like pulling drum layers into phase alignment or for musical things like giving a snare track a slightly lazy feel.

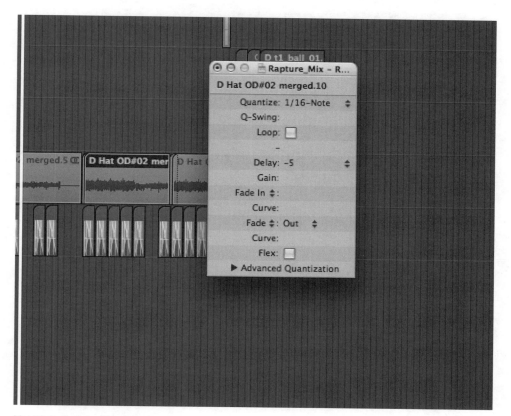

Mat Mitchell's Delay Time adjustment

The Oldest Trick in the Logic Book of Grooves: Option + Scissors

Let's close out this chapter with an all-time favorite technique for building a drum groove and by introducing that sense of "the drummer getting busy." This is the only situation in which I still recommend using the Scissors tool—now otherwise obsolete since the invention of Logic's Marquee tool for cutting.

- Start with a perfectly looping drum loop, and zoom in tight on a region.
- Hold down the Option key. Wherever you place the Scissors tool within the region, equal slices of the same duration in time will be created.
- For example, cut into a region after one quarter-note beat to make four even slices, cut into a region after an eighth note to make eight slices, and so on.
- These perfectly timed slivers of the beat can be muted, copied, and otherwise rearranged to create infinite variations to the groove.
- A favorite place to start is to create an eighth-note or 16th-note sliver out of the Kick, and then paste four in a row at the end of the region for a stutter effect.

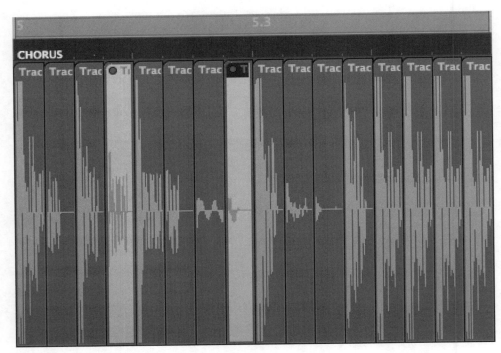

Option + Scissors beat slicing

Check out the Option + Scissors example on the accompanying DVD-ROM in Tutorial #1, "Programming Drums," and make sure to use this tool every day for at least a few days so that it becomes automatic. In fact, as an exercise, use a few tools from this chapter every day as a new starting point in your writing or as a turning point to achieve that sense of completion to your Logic projects. Not every Logic idea you start will get finished, but with a few of these tools hopefully more of your ideas can reach that point of satisfaction.

Chapter 10

ESPECIALLY FOR COMPOSERS

(AND ARRANGERS IN THE MODERN WORLD)

L ogic has a long history behind its reputation as a scoring program. It was the next generation of software from the makers of Notator SL for the Atari computer, and Notator was world renowned for its scoring prowess. Logic Pro is simply deeper and more flexible and has more editing power than Notator ever did, but the foundation for creating full orchestral scores, lead sheets, and charts was laid before Logic was even born. A complete introduction to creating musical scores is well beyond the scope of this book and is covered in the manual. Below are a few of the fundamental concepts and some handy tricks for projects involving live musicians who read music and charts.

This chapter also covers a number of tools specifically for film composing, such as working with video in Logic, SMPTE lock, and so on.

The second half of this chapter is intended for all Logic users who are ready to develop their Logic project's appearance and arrangement with the same attention to detail of the traditional composer. Music itself continues to evolve through the evolution of the tools. Logic has a wide array of these newer tools designed to foster musical development and arrangement. These tools and techniques bring a sense of graphic organization to your work that I guarantee will inspire your creative workflow.

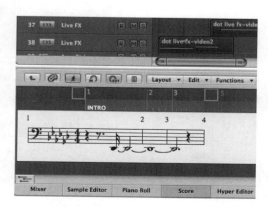

The Score Editor

Tapping into the Score Editor

The Score is available from the tab at the bottom of the Arrange window or at the top of the Arrange window from the Windows menu (Window > Score). Either way it defaults to the notation of whatever track is highlighted.

Once the Score is open, double-click on the background to view and edit the notation for the whole arrangement (and not just one instrument). For the reverse results—to isolate the notation for just the track you're working on—double-click on an instrument's music staff.

Power Tip: Duration Bars in the View Menu

There are many detailed tools available in the View menu to explore. Refer to the Help files for a full description, but as an example, turn on the Duration Bars (Score > View > Duration Bars) to edit note length in the score.

Real-Time Scoring Transcription

While you program MIDI data, your score is transcribed in real time in the Score editor. Be sure that the yellow chain-link icon is enabled, or the Score will not update to link to the track selected in the Arrange window. That can be convenient if, for example, you prefer to view the Score from a previous performance of a bass line or chord progression while you input a solo.

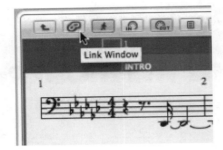

Link windows

Creating a Lead Sheet Automatically

This is a very cool way to quickly create a lead sheet for the band.

- Enable the Chord track within global tracks in the Arrange window.
- Highlight a software instrument track with MIDI data containing a chord progression.
- Select Analyze in the track header of the global track.
- Logic will calculate and display the chord progression of your performance.
- Switch to view the Score Editor. Notice that the chords appear in the Score by choosing Score Editor > Select Functions > Insert Chords From Chord Global Track.
- Be sure that you have the correct music staff selected in the Score Editor before selecting to insert.

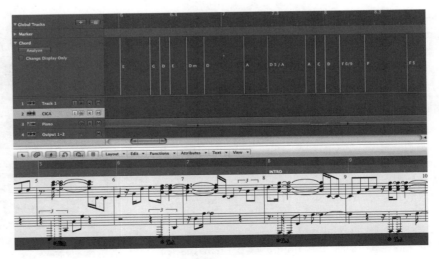

Global Chord Track to analyze chord progression

Text Tool for Inputting Lyrics

Enable the Text tool by selecting the Lyric mode in the parameter box on the left, beneath the Instrument Set Parameter box. Then select the Text tool from the toolbox in the upper left or with the Escape key. While you enter lyrics, the Tab key will move you to the next note event in the score.

Instrument Sets to Merge Score of Independent Regions

Instrument Sets allow you to view at once an entire track that has independent regions. Otherwise, when you click on the Score Editor, you may be confused that you see notation of only two bars, for example.

- Highlight a track in the Arrange window so that all its regions are selected in Arrange area.
- In the Score Editor, select Layout > Create Instrument Set From Selection.
- To view all Instrument Sets when multiple instruments are in an arrangement, select from the top of the parameter boxes in Score Inspector > All Sets.

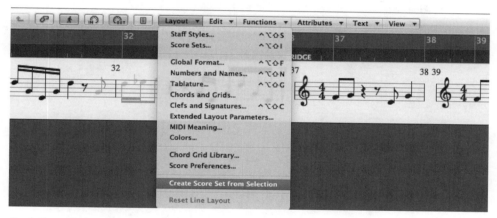

Create Score Set to merge view of all regions

The Instrument Set Parameter Box and the Part Box

Beneath the menu of Instrument Sets is the Instrument Set Parameter box. This is located where the Region Parameter box is found in the Arrange window. Here you can choose the Score Style for each Instrument Set independently (whether for Guitar, Piano, Violin, Drums, and so on) from the top pull-down menu labeled Style. Double-click on the Style name to open a detailed view of its score, such as Staff, Clef, Spacing and so on. Soprano Sax is used in the example below.

Score Style for each Instrument Set

Drag-and-drop elements from the Part box in the Score window inspector into the Score workspace to embellish your notation.

Global Score Project Settings

Here you can make detailed definitions to your score, such as changing the spacing between notes and bars per line. From the Settings menu in the toolbar, select Score (Settings > Score). The detail here for everything from Signatures to Guitar Tablature is phenomenal, considering its integration with MIDI and audio recording via the Audio To Score feature.

Global Score Settings

Printing Your Score

You can print your score directly from within Logic once you fine-tune your score layout. It's a great way to examine any spacing or labeling issues needing refinement. Even if you're not a composer or an arranger needing a printed score for live musicians, you may enjoy having a hard-copy, traditional score of your Logic project.

- Enable the Page View button on top of the local Score Editor to see the print view. It's the button to the right of the MIDI Out button, labeled Page View when you hover over it with your mouse.
- Select File > Print from the Arrange window.

Page View button

Film-Scoring Hurdles of SMPTE and Sync

In addition to the QuickTime window (File > Open movie), there is a Video track in the global tracks for a linear view of thumbnails of the video while you're working on an arrangement. This can be helpful for visually anticipating shots in the timeline.

SMPTE Offsets, Picture Sync, and Other Fun Stuff

Synchronization between Logic and picture admittedly can feel like a brainteaser, but it's not rocket science. The basic task is lining up SMPTE start times between an imported QuickTime movie and Logic's bar ruler. If you import a movie with a different SMPTE start time, go to Song Settings > Synchronization, where you can type in a new start time.

The Enable Separate SMPTE View offset allows you to change the way time it is displayed in the transport. You can make the transport display zero at the song start, rather than the true SMPTE start time. In other words, you would enter the actual SMPTE time you want Logic to start at in the Plays At SMPTE field, and the Displayed At SMPTE time you want to see in the offset field. So if you want Logic to start playing when it sees, say, 1:00:01:00, but want it to display 0:00:00.00, you would enter those times in the respective fields.

It gets a bit tricky if you need to synchronize an external video camera or other video playback device with Logic. You will need a MIDI interface or third-party converter to convert SMPTE to MTC (MIDI Time Code) to lock any external video

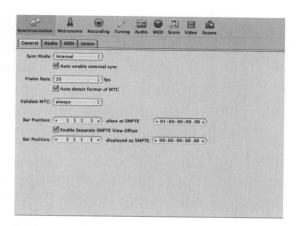

Synchronization Settings for SMPTE start

camera or player with Logic. A detail to be aware of in general with SMPTE is that it is quarter-frame, not sample-accurate—there are 4 data bytes per SMPTE frame with MIDI Time Code.

Spotting to Picture: Dropping FX at SMPTE Locations

While Logic is not typically the application for postproduction engineers responsible for spotting to picture (dropping sound effects at exact SMPTE locations), there are great tools for doing this in Logic. If you are working with movies as a film composer, these tools will come in handy.

Move the playhead to an exact bar or SMPTE position where you'd like to place a sound effect, vocal, or other audio file.

Ctrl-click on the audio file from the Standalone Audio Bin (Arrange > Window > Audio Bin) to directly at the playhead position. Note: This Audio Bin is separate from the Bin integrated in the Media area of the Arrange window.

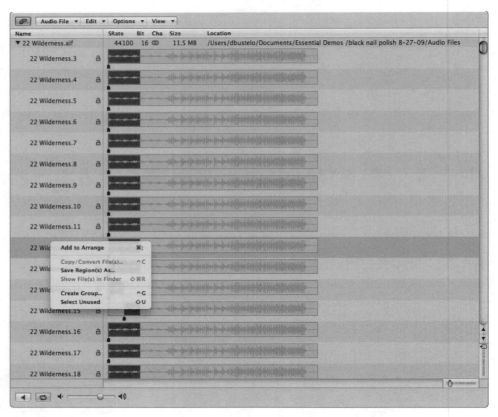

Standalone Audio Bin for spotting

To view SMPTE in the bar ruler, click in the upper right of Arrange window beneath the toolbar, directly to the right of the bar ruler. There is a thin vertical bar of musical notes to enable the view of Bar and Time.

You can navigate to an exact position in time in the Event List, and then drop a note event at that location.

- Go to Lists in the upper right of the toolbar.
- Select the Event tab.
- In the Event List, select View > Event Position and Length in SMPTE Units.

- Highlight the desired note event in the Event List. Audition by selecting.
- Optional: Open the Piano Roll to see the highlighted note event in the Event List.
- Select the key command called Pickup Clock (Move Event to Playhead Position) assigned to the semi-colon ";" by default.
- The event will move to the playhead.

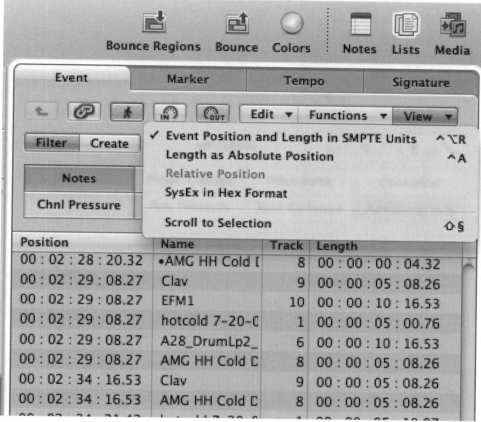

The Event List

Classic and Modern Arranging Techniques

Every Logic user should know the following arranging techniques and use them regularly.

Power Moves for Building the Arrangement

Setting locators and cycling sections. The left and right locators refer to the in and out points, respectively, of a Cycle section that is defined in the bar ruler. You can type in these values in the transport or drag in the bar ruler to extend or shorten an existing cycle. Cycle can be enabled or disabled in the transport, but it's likely something you'll do from a key command since you'll be toggling on and off so often.

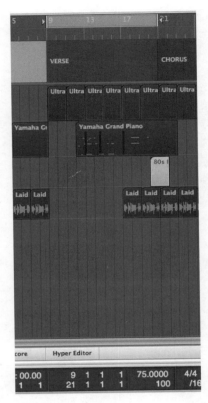

The Cycle area and the locators

Using Skip Cycle to audition alternate arrangements. When you swipe backward in the bar ruler over a cycle section, the cycle indication turns from solid shaded green to what is sometimes referred to as a candy cane or barbershop pole appearance. When you play back the project, Logic will skip over this area, allowing you to preview the arrangement without the defined bars. Maybe you want to explore shortening a chorus or breakdown. A popular request, which is unfortunately not possible, is to be able to bounce your project without the Skip Cycle section. Even if Skip Cycle is enabled, Logic will still include that area in a project bounce.

Skip Cycle

Cutting and inserting time. Using these two tools should become second nature to you while building your Logic arrangement. Define an area by the locators in the bar ruler. Make sure that all desired tracks are highlighted. Then from the Edit menu in the Arrange window, select the desired action in the subfolder to Cut/Insert Time (Edit > Cut/Insert Time).

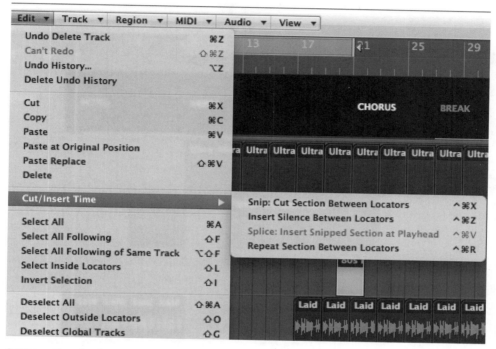

Cutting and inserting time

Repeating a section. There is a great tool in the toolbar appropriately called Repeat Section that you can use to repeat the area defined by the locators of a cycled area. All the tracks in the area defined by the locators will repeat directly after the cycle area ends. This tool is also an option in the Edit menu explained above for cutting and inserting time (Edit > Cut/Insert Time > Repeat Section Between Locators).

Setting your song length. You can define the length of your Logic project in the transport by typing in the value beneath in the tempo. If this value isn't defined, certain operations like bouncing a track will continue for what seems like forever! There is also an indication in the bar ruler of the end of song—the small rectangle in the upper half of the bar ruler. Drag on this directly to adjust the song length.

Project Length in transport

Making Your Project Look Good

The scores written by Mozart and Beethoven remain visual works of art even hundreds of years after they were written. There are many Logic tools that honor the tradition of creating a visual masterpiece by introducing modern attributes like color-coding to its presentation.

It's all about the markers. The value of using markers cannot be stated enough. Markers are created in the global Marker track in the Arrange window (Global Tracks > Marker). If the Marker track is not in view, click-and-hold on the track header in the global tracks, and check the box next to Markers.

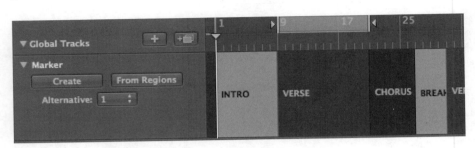

The Marker track in the global tracks

Once the Marker track is visible, you can move your playhead to the desired location and then click in the track list, on the button labeled Create Marker. The default name will be Marker 1, Marker 2, and so on. Double-click on that name or Ctrl-click into the marker area to rename (for example, as Intro, Verse, Chorus, Break, and so on).

To change the beginning or end point of a marker, drag on the left or right corner of the marker. The Pointer tool will turn into a bracket-shaped tool allowing you to make these length adjustments.

Here's where it gets visually satisfying. You can colorize the markers with the Color tool in the toolbar or by using the key command to open the Color Palette. This really helps your eye keep up with the arrangement as it evolves. Maybe all the verses or the A section will be blue and the choruses or B section will be light blue.

When you collapse the Marker track, the markers remain visible in the lower half of the bar ruler. You may decide you need the screen real estate and that it's best to keep the markers small inside the bar ruler. On the other hand, you might like keeping the Marker track open for the additional editing purposes. When the markers are visible only in the lower half of the bar ruler, you cannot drag on their start or end point to adjust, rename, and the like.

Markers in bar ruler

Coloring tracks for mood and practical considerations. Coloring tracks is just like coloring markers. Use the Color tool in the toolbar or the key command to open the Color Palette, then start coloring. The color scheme you choose is entirely personal and should reflect a combination of your aesthetic and your practical needs for organizing tracks in your project. Some users follow a similar color scheme in all their sessions: for example, software instruments are blue, audio tracks are red. Or, all tracks are just a fruit salad of colors. Mine tend to be colored quite deliberately to reflect the mood at the time of creation of the particular Logic project—sometimes the colors of the season, but somehow the mood of the project itself. The color scheme tends to be refined as I develop the project. It's as though I'm my own art director designing the look that the music expresses. And of course the track color and marker color are always well coordinated. Musicians are often wowed when they see my projects, and start coloring their own sessions with the same pride and excitement about the new look of their projects.

Changing the track icon. The icon to the left of the track name in the track list can be adjusted. I'll be honest—I don't personally change these often, but it is visually stimulating when you do and can help with keeping track of a large session. To change the icon, highlight the track header in the track list. You'll then find the icon in the Inspector to the left, in the Instrument Parameter box in the middle of the column.

It makes sense that the track icon is selected here, since these are parameters relevant to the entire Instrument, not an individual region. Click-and-hold on the icon to open up a full-screen menu of other icons you can choose from. Click on the desired one to select it.

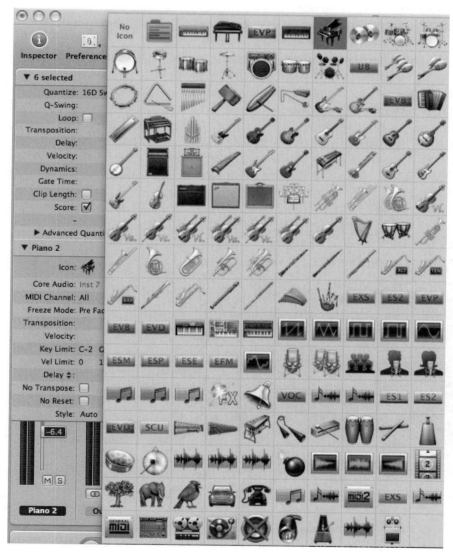

Instrument Icon menu

Configuring the track header. Ctrl-click on the track header in the track list to open a menu of which components you want visible in the track list.

Screensets. Screensets were at the heart of early Logic, before the one-window interface became the core of the Logic workflow. Screensets allow you to customize your workspace and basically lock into view the editor or multiple editors and the size of objects in the window. Now, of course, the Arrange window is where most of the real creation work is done, and all other editors and assets are simply a click away— especially now that the Mixer is always partially in view with the dual channel strip design.

Screensets still can be quite practical. Sometimes there is a lot going on—between plug-ins open and editors in view at a very specific zoom level—and it's helpful to lock in the view via a screenset. A screenset gets saved to each numeric key on your computer keyboard (1, 2, 3, and so on), and is then recalled by selecting that specific numeric key. That way you can return to it while working on the complicated tasks at hand. To create a screenset:

- Use the numeric keyboard above alphabet keys to select the number to assign to the screenset. If necessary, first select Screenset > Unlock, then Lock.
- Rearrange and resize editors and other objects as you wish to see them (for example, plug-in windows, secondary editors, track size, and so on).
- Save the view as a screenset by selecting Screenset > Lock at the top of the Arrange window.

A locked screenset will have a bullet next to the screenset number, meaning that if you temporarily resize your window or delete something in view, the next time you select the designated screenset with its number key on your keyboard, the saved screenset will be placed in view. In the diagram below, Screenset 2 is locked in with the Piano Roll editor in view; no Inspector and no Media area is visible on the right displaying Apple Loops or channel strip settings in order to maximize the Edit and Arrange areas.

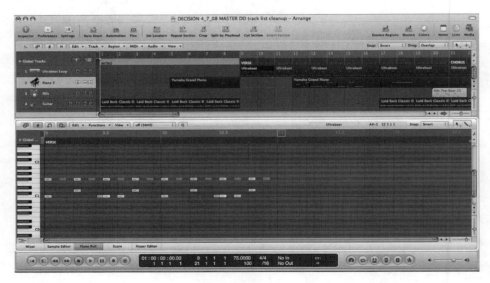

A locked screenset

Sometimes a highly creative or technical moment in Logic feels like a complex puzzle. Just being able to control what and how you view the musical events can help jump-start your Logic brain to see you through. Think of it like moving things around physically in your studio in order to feel optimized and focused: your keyboard, your mouse, your chair, maybe even your beverage. The idea with Logic is to feel in control of your personal studio workspace.

In the past Logic was all about customizing which editors opened and saving these window configurations as screensets that were accessed from the numeric keys on the keyboard. The idea was to make your Logic workspace conform to your workflow. You can still do this (see chapter 11, "Good Housekeeping and Other Smart Practices"). Logic is still infinitely customizable, which is part of its elegance and legacy. However, the simplicity of Logic's one-window interface encourages minimal customization— not to mention minimal confusion—when you walk into someone else's Logic studio.

In the past, I obsessed over creating screensets—resizing editors and placing objects in specific places on the Logic screen—designing my virtual studio like a physical studio. Now I do a few things like coloring markers and tracks to create a signature look and mood to each of my Logic sessions. Otherwise, I rely on the default view settings.

Chapter 11
GOOD HOUSEKEEPING
(AND OTHER SMART PRACTICES)

Keeping a clean, tidy, and organized digital studio is at the core of enjoying your experience as a Logic user. You can still create great music without applying these practices, but you may have more headaches from losing critical files and wasting time with inefficient and lazy workflow habits.

Managing Your Logic Project

This was introduced in chapter 3, "Writing Your First Track in Logic," but it is important enough to discuss again. Logic song files are automatically saved into a Logic project folder with all the related assets of the project. The application is trying to direct you to practice good housekeeping and keep everything in one place, including your EXS24 instruments and their associated samples (also the Ultrabeat samples).

A common error is to forget to enable the inner checkboxes of the Advanced Options in the Assets folder. Without these checked, the associated samples are not included in the project folder. It is your choice whether to include the samples, but keeping them in one project folder means that you will always have those drum samples and violin samples you need for the song to play back properly on another computer or at another studio. All of your Logic project folders should be backed up in at least two places. "It's not backed up if it's not backed up twice" is a truism that should be emblazoned in your mind. This is the best way to ensure that you always have a backup.

If you are using a third-party sampler, keep in mind that those samples will need to be manually saved if you want your Logic project to open properly in another studio.

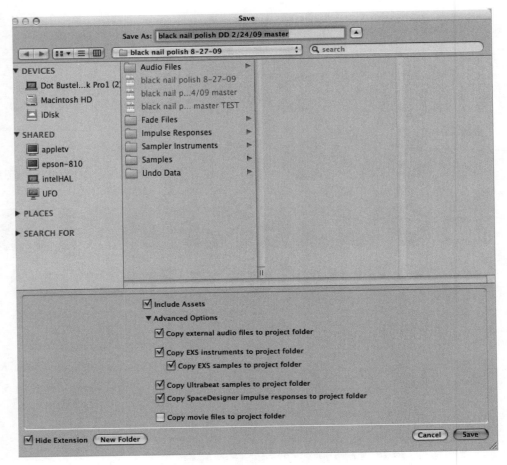

The Logic project folder

When viewing from the Finder, the Logic song file is the file with an icon of a music keyboard, within the project folder.

Logic song file

Understanding How to Bounce

Bouncing audio files consolidates the tracks with all the effects plug-ins so they can be played back universally outside of the DAW or perhaps conserve CPU resources if needed.

Bouncing the Master File

Logic nailed it with the bounce options. You access the Bounce menu from either the bottom of the Main Output channel strip, the File menu in the Arrange window (File >

Bounce), or the Bounce tool in the toolbar. All three bring up the same dialog box. In the Bounce menu you can select between real-time or offline, which is much faster at no loss of quality. Offline makes sense if you don't need to hear the final mix while it's bouncing, and would actually prefer to rest your ears.

The bounces by default are placed in a Bounce folder within the Logic project folder. In the Bounce dialog box, you are free to redirect the path to anywhere on your hard drive. You may prefer keeping all your bounces in one location, for example.

In the Bounce dialog box you can also choose to create an MP3 at the same time and enable the checkbox to send it directly to your iTunes library, which is pretty awesome. You can also burn directly to a CD, which does require a real-time—not offline—bounce.

Bounce in Place

A longtime request of Logic users has finally been honored. You can select to bounce in place an individual region or an entire track from the local region and track menus in the Arrange window for any highlighted region or track (Track > Bounce Track in Place). The dialog box that opens allows you to choose whether to create a new track for the bounce and mute the original, or replace it. You also have the option to include or not include any effects plug-ins on the track. Pretty handy and versatile, depending on what the bounce will be used for.

Bounce in Place

Project Templates

Back in the day, there was the Autoload. This was the default Logic song file you created as your starting point for every new Logic project. Logic users spent a lot of time designing their Autoload to include cabling to their external hardware synthesizers. When software instruments were introduced, many users added to their Autoload a palette of favorite sounds: favorite acoustic piano, favorite bass sound, favorite drum kit, and so on. In fact some professional Logic users had multiple Autoloads depending on what sort of project they were starting (a dance track, a pop song, and so on). If you are speaking to a longtime Logic user, they are likely to still refer to their default song as an Autoload, but Logic has renamed these as project templates to be more generic and encourage the idea that you can have multiple project templates depending on the type of project you are starting.

File   Edit   Options   Window

New...   ⌘N
Open...   ⌘O
Open Recent   ▶

Close   ⌘W
Close Project   ⌥⌘W
Save   ⌘S
Save As...   ⇧⌘S
Save A Copy As...
Save as Template...

Creating a project template

There are some great factory templates that you may want to check out for different situations like Surround Production or Multi-Track Production. There are also some great templates by musical genre with various software instruments and effects plug-ins that are preloaded (for example, Electronic, Orchestral, and so on) that may be a good starting point for creating your own project templates.

To create a project template, simply start with an empty project, then open whatever instruments or plug-ins or number of empty audio or software instrument tracks you like to see when you get started, and then select from the File menu > Save As Template.

Setting Up Patch Names for Analog Keyboards: Multi-Instruments

This is the solution for the task of storing the patch names of external MIDI hardware used by your song within the Logic project. Logic does not support the Audio MIDI Setup Utility's .midnam files that Pro Tools and Digital Performer do.

This is the only setup activity you may still need to do in the Environment. The Multi-Instruments section allows you to store the patch (program) names of your hardware synthesizers inside Logic in your empty project template so that you can save and recall individual patch names. The good news is that many of the popular MIDI keyboards have multi-instruments already created and passed around online, which are perfectly fine to use. You don't have to type in all the patch names and bank messages from the keyboard manual.

Launch the Environment (Window > Environment), and then select the MIDI Inst layer in the upper left of the window. This menu is located where the Region Parameter box is found in the Arrange window.

If you have a multi-instrument for your keyboard that you maybe found online or had on another computer, copy/paste it into the MIDI Environment layer and highlight the object. In the parameter box on the left, tell Logic which MIDI port it's cabled to on your MIDI interface.

Next, enable all 16 MIDI channels by clicking on the slashes through the "Hollywood Squares"–type template for each subchannel.

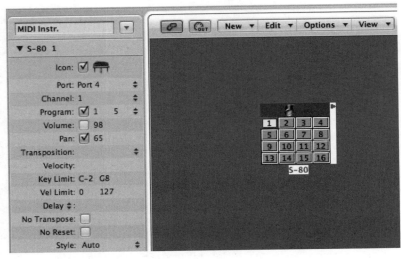

Multi-Instrument in MIDI Environment

Back in the Arrange window, select the keyboard by name from the External Instrument on a software instrument track (see chapter 7, "Creating with Logic's Software Instruments," for details on the External Instrument). If you do not have a multi-instrument for a particular instrument, go to the local menu labeled New and select Multi-Instrument if it is, or Instrument if it's a monophonic instrument that plays on only one MIDI channel (like a Roland Juno-106). Rename the object by clicking on the default name beneath the icon.

Backing Up Your Presets and Settings

Any settings you create in Logic (channel strip settings, Plug-in Settings, Space Designer IRs, and so on) are all placed in the Logic folder in the Application Support folder of your Home folder. This Logic folder should be backed up—and that means backed up in *two* places—for safekeeping. This is also the folder that you will want to keep consistent between all of your computers so that you always have all your plug-in settings. This file path should become very familiar to you.

The Logic folder from the Finder view

Marker Text "TelePrompter" on Second Monitor

Many power Logic users swear by marker text view for live shows, even dragging it to a second monitor. You can drag any editor to a second monitor that's connected to your computer by manually dragging it with your mouse off of one monitor until it "catches" on the second monitor.

Mat Mitchell names marker text as one of his favorite creative tools in Logic:

> I use this quite a bit for tracking—a Floating Marker list on a second display visible to the performer. You can fit quite a bit of information in this window. I'll put things like song lyrics, positions, or reminders such as "1/2-time section in 4 beats."

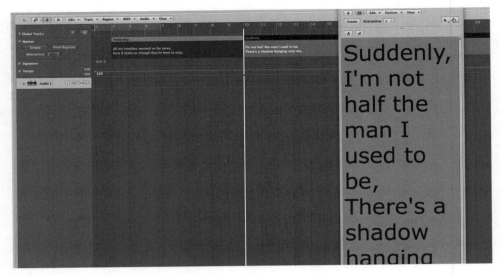

Marker text from Mat Mitchell

Making Notes in Your Project

This is a cool feature in Logic. You can create a text file within the project for your notes. These may be about the plug-in settings used, mix levels, or even different vocal takes still under consideration.

You create your notes with the Notes tool in the toolbar at the upper right of the Arrange window. When you select Notes, there are two tabs to choose from: global for the project or per track. The Notes window allows you to even pick the font and font size.

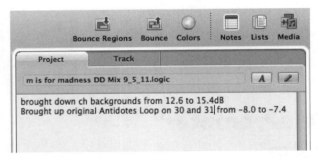

Project Notes in the toolbar

Optimizing Your System Performance

There is an audio preference that you can adjust to save on CPU resources (Preferences > Audio > General > Track Mute/Solo > "CPU-saving" mode). When this is selected, muting a track will mute the plug-ins on the channel strip and free up system resources for other tasks.

Chapter 12
TROUBLE-SHOOTING

Best Practices

Troubleshooting can feel like shooting in the dark, when in actuality there is a science to it and an empowering skill that you can develop. There is a satisfying sense of accomplishment when you do resolve an issue in the studio, even if it has meant losing an hour or a whole day of time you didn't have. If something isn't working properly, there's quite likely a reason for it that you can isolate. Sometimes it is an intermittent bug in the software or hardware you've encountered, but even that is likely documented online.

Be methodical and leave no stone unturned in any troubleshooting mission. As quoted by Grammy winner and engineer Dave Darlington in this book's introduction and worth repeating again here: "The machines don't win. People do!" Every link in your studio that could be directly or indirectly causing the problem needs to be examined, from a cracked plug-in to a MIDI controller with an old driver that starts acting up after you run a software update. The Internet has become your greatest tool for troubleshooting. You no longer have to wait until morning to reach out for help. No matter the hour, you are not alone between manufacturer websites and user forums. Inevitably someone else has had the same problem and received the same error message or crash, or you can post your own issue.

Without documenting every problem that may arise, this chapter will introduce a few best practices when it comes to resolving issues in the studio, especially in your Logic studio. Most importantly, never get lazy or so frustrated in your troubleshooting mission that you skip a step that could lead to the critical discovery.

The Scene of the Crime

Always be self-aware when you working in Logic, no matter how lost creatively you may get in the music. When a problem arises—whether a cryptic error message, a system overload, or a system crash—you want to be able to document precisely the scene of the Logic accident and everything you were doing up to that point (that is, were you editing, playing back audio, recording or loading a particular plug-in?). Ideally, for any effective technical support, you will be able to explain what was going on in your studio, if not how to reproduce the problem.

The Crash Log

System crashes may be the most annoying, inconvenient, and stressful of all. If you've been diligently saving and backing up as you work, a crash will at least not be deadly. However, having to reboot Logic or possibly the computer itself derails the creative process, and an emerging musical idea may be lost forever. To help avoid the reoccurrence of the same crash, you will need to know what happened, and when it happened, in order to research its cause—and Logic gives you tools to do this.

The next time Logic crashes, hit the Report button if the dialog box appears before the machine freezes and you have to force quit. Instead of selecting to report to Apple, select to save the Crash Log; it can often be revealing about the source of the crash. The long text log will look like illegible DOS computer language. If you scan, you may find key words repeated that indicate either a system conflict with something third party or something within the computer itself that provides a clue (for example, ReWire Instrument, Airport Wireless, Digidesign Midi Driver, and so on). Sometimes there can be an old driver or resource on your computer from a forgotten piece of hardware or software that you don't even use that's causing a conflict. If you're not able to grab the Crash Log at the scene of the crash, there is a Crash Log file that you can investigate from the Finder: ~/Library/Logs/Crash Reporter/Logic Pro.crash.log

Power Tip: Taking a Snapshot of Your Screen

Remembering the exact wording of an error message dialog box is also not easy; they seem to have a language unto themselves and offer no insight into the problem. It's as though code writers are talking to themselves—not to you, the user.

For troubleshooting purposes of searching online for answers, take a snapshot of the specific area on your screen that has the error message by holding down Shift + Command + 4. Shift + Command + 3 will take a picture of your entire screen. Try it now if you haven't used these keystrokes before.

If you need to research online or speak to an expert friend or even Apple, you will need to know the following:

- Your System Specs: what model computer, what operating system, what version of Logic, what audio interface, what third-party plug-ins you are using.
- What you were doing when the problem or crash occurred.
- Did the problem happen in one session only, or can you reproduce it in other sessions?

Avoiding Latency While Recording and System Overloads

The I/O buffer size setting in your Audio preferences is intended to be a dynamic setting. This means it is one that you adjust depending on what task you are doing. "I/O" refers to input/output, as far as digital audio. If you are recording, you want to bring this setting down to as low a value as possible, whether 64 or even 32 so that the live musician or singer experiences little latency.

When you have a high-quality audio interface, latency is easily controlled with a small buffer size, without introducing any crackling or other unacceptable noise. This takes more CPU resources, so when you need more system resources for plug-ins, you may want to increase this value all the way up to even 1,024. Whether you are in the writing or the mixing stage—layering plug-ins and swapping out virtual instruments sometimes for more CPU-intensive ones—you may find that the System Overload message shows its ugly head. If you are receiving System Overload messages, that's a good indication that you may need to increase the I/O buffer size. The adjustment to the buffer size does not take place until you select Apply Changes, in the lower right of screen.

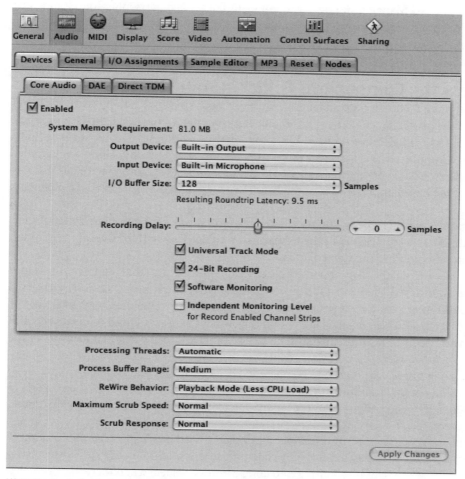

I/O buffer size in the Audio preferences

Problems with Third-Party Plug-Ins

For better or worse, Logic's own plug-ins seem to be the most stable and efficient in Logic. Logic plug-ins are a collection of plug-ins made by the same development team making the DAW itself, so it makes sense that they have this stability. That said, the palette of third-party instruments and effects are well worth the occasional challenges.

Audio Units and the Audio Unit Manager

Audio Units are a system-level architecture of plug-ins developed for OS X for third-party plug-in manufacturers. The Audio Unit protocol was designed to be as efficient as possible with the lowest possible latency within OS X, compared with other protocols like VST developed years ago by Steinberg. Third-party developers are part of the Apple developer community. They receive access to a new operating system before it is released on the Mac, to give them time to build any essential updates to their plug-ins, generally made available on their respective websites.

The Audio Units Manager is similar to a Mac utility but is built directly into Logic to manage the third-party plug-ins being used by Logic. This was covered in the section "Adding Third-Party Software Instruments" in chapter 1, but again, you may need to launch the AU Manager in Logic after an install of a third-party plug-in to jump-start them to be recognized by Logic (Arrange > Preferences > Audio Units Manager).

Make sure that any troublesome plug-in is actually on the list and that its checkbox is enabled for Logic, then hit the Reset & Rescan Selection button.

Know the Components Folder in Your Finder

If you have reoccurring problems with your Logic studio, not to point fingers, but there is a good chance it could be emanating from one of these third-party plug-ins. Third-party plug-ins recognized by Logic must be of the Audio Unit format. Logic has not supported VSTs since the OS X operating system. Audio Units are installed globally and will work once installed in both Logic and GarageBand, as well as in many other Mac-based applications. Audio Units live on your hard drive in the Components folder.

Audio Units may be in the root level of your computer, or in your Home folder. In either case, they reside in the Components folder in a path of the Library folder: Library/Audio/Plug-Ins/Components.

Remove from the Components folder any Audio Units that you are not really using (Library > Audio > Plug-Ins > Components). To remove, just drag them to the desktop or create another safe folder for them on the same directory level, maybe called "Unused Components" or "X-Components". There is no need to delete them. If you want to use one of them again, just slide it back into the original location in the Components folder.

You don't necessarily need to be immediately drastic and remove them all, but keep that as an option if nothing else helps. At that point remove all of them, then add them back one by one until you can reproduce the crashing. This can be time-consuming, but effective.

Also make sure that plug-ins are updated from their respective manufacturer websites. This naturally applies only to legitimate plug-ins you have purchased. Keep in mind that any troubleshooting and compatibility issues, when there are problems with your system, apply only to legitimate products. No QA or technical support teams are testing cracks!

The Components view from the Finder

Audio MIDI Setup Utility

If you are having problems with audio or MIDI communication with any external hardware, this Mac utility is a good place to start to check whether your computer is even recognizing the gear. As mentioned in chapter 1, "Setting Up Your Logic Studio," I refer to this utility so often that I leave it in the dock as well as the Finder Places for easy access.

There are separate tabs for any audio and MIDI equipment with drivers installed on your computer. If a piece of your hardware is on the list but grayed out, you know right away your computer is not recognizing it, and the problem is not isolated to Logic. It could be a physical problem with the cabling (for example, the unit is not plugged in) or it could be driver related. If the latter is the case, check the manufacturer's website and see if there is an updated driver to download and install.

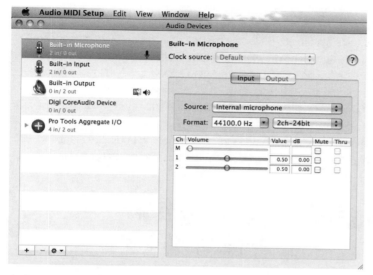

Audio MIDI Setup utility

Trashing Your Logic Preferences

The following is a tried-and-true troubleshooting technique for many ailments in Logic. Navigate from the Finder to your Preference folder, and then delete the relevant Logic preference files, all located in the file path Home Folder > Library > Preferences > "com.apple.logic…"

Logic will rebuild its Preferences the next time you launch the app. There are three Logic preferences in this folder to remove if Logic is acting up. After you remove the Preference files, it's best to restart your computer to really flush the system. Keep in mind that any Preference assignments you've made will have to be reentered when you launch Logic (that is, assigning your audio hardware in the Audio preferences, General Editing preferences, and so on).

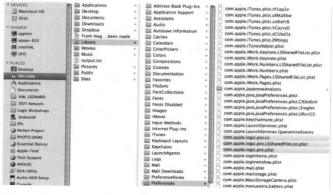

Logic preferences view from the Finder

If you have customized your key commands (see chapter 6, "The Secret to Learning Logic: Key Commands"), there is the option to initialize all your Logic preferences except for the key commands. From the Preferences menu in the Arrange window, select Initialize All Except Key Commands.

Miscellaneous Troubleshooting Tricks

- Refresh graphics: Click between areas of the Arrange window to redraw the screen.
- Switch to "Built-in" Core Audio: If you suspect the audio interface driver might be the culprit, work with the Mac's built-in sound for a while to see if the problem disappears. Or, start Logic without any audio engine. Hold down the Ctrl key immediately after launching Logic. When the option to launch Core Audio appears, say "No".
- Start Logic without opening a project: Hold down the Option key immediately after launching Logic to bypass loading any project that automatically loads as a result of your Startup Action preference.
- Start Logic in AU-safe mode: If you are having trouble launching Logic, try disabling unvalidated Audio Unit plug-ins by holding down Shift + Ctrl immediately after launching Logic.

Facing a Logic Song Corruption

It just happens. The Logic song files themselves can get corrupted or damaged, like anything else in the world that can break. It is just data. This is, of course, why we back up—twice.

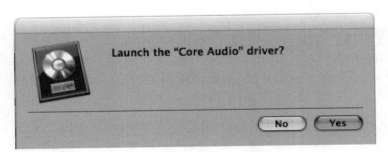

Ctrl key launch to bypass the audio driver

If you find yourself in a situation where you don't have a proper backup (for example, a song you wrote before you knew better), you have a few choices as far as salvaging parts of your work. Try launching Logic without the Audio driver by holding down the Ctrl key during launch of the app. You will get a dialog box asking if you want to launch the "Core Audio" driver. You should select "no". This way, if the corruption was with the audio portion of the Logic project you can at least open the song file.

By bypassing the audio driver, you can potentially open and at least see the MIDI files of the project. Then, either copy-and-paste manually the MIDI data to a fresh Logic project or use the File > Export Selection As MIDI File in the Arrange window. Then, you can try bringing in the audio files to the new session, possibly using the Track Import function.

Slaving Your MPC

The Akai MPC drum machine remains a mainstay in many production rooms. This is true even though many newer beat machines in the form of plug-ins and hardware controllers are on the market, which have surpassed the MPC workflow in features and efficiency. Still to this day, the MPC has a loyal following of A-list commercial producers and beat makers who continue to integrate an MPC with Logic in a variety of ways.

The first rule of thumb is that your computer should always be your master sequencer and external drum machines, including the Akai MPC, should slave to Logic—or any computer-based DAW for that matter. Think of a standalone drum machine being the master clock to a computer, like a pony pulling a double-decker bus. The best advice is to follow the example of a Logic user like Jay Z's engineer, Young Guru, who advanced his MPC workflow to simply importing his MPC groove templates into Logic (see chapter 9, "Remixing and Making Beats").

Keep in mind that Logic has not been able to slave to MIDI Clock since version 7, a source of great frustration to many Logic users still wanting to use a drum machine as the master sequencer.

Another related production practice, again not advised though possible, is using the MPC as the master sequencer and using Logic essentially as a giant instrument (technically a multi-instrument)—not using the Logic sequencer at all.

To use Logic as a 16-channel multi-instrument (the number of channels in the MIDI standard), a common problem experienced by users is to find Logic playing back on only one channel, not all 16 independently.

There are two steps to remedy this. First, set the MIDI channel in the Instrument Parameter box, in the middle of the left-hand column of the Arrange window (the Inspector column) for each software instrument track.

The second and essential step is to enable the "Auto Demix by Channel if Multi-track Recording" in the Recording Settings.

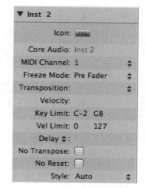

Assign MIDI channel in Instrument Parameter box

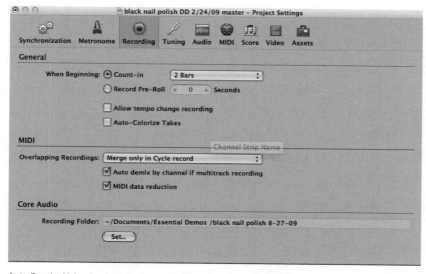

Auto Demix: Using Logic as instrument with external sequencer

Then, if you want the Logic instrument to receive on all 16 channels, set the Multi-Instrument's MIDI channel in the Instrument Parameter box to All.

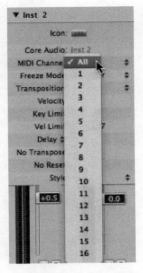

"All" MIDI Channel to receive on all16 channels

At the End of the Day

At the end of the day, there is no right or wrong to a Logic workflow. It is truly whatever makes you be creative and productive. Your workflow may be incredibly inefficient or downright wrong to a trained recording engineer. I've seen plenty of Logic projects of hit songs with enough faux pas to give Logic developers a coronary attack. But creating in Logic is not open-heart surgery. Music itself and certainly Logic is yours to do with as you please. Hopefully this book has helped you along your path of becoming one with Logic so that your music evolves and you can enjoy the process just a little bit more along the way.

APPENDIX A:
DOT'S KEY COMMANDS
IN LOGIC

Here are the Logic key commands that substantially speed up my personal workflow. These commands were not default assignments but ones that felt "logical" to me. So, I customized the keystroke combinations. See chapter 6 for the following:

- Getting instructions regarding how to customize your own key commands
- Finding out what a keystroke combination is assigned to
- Learning how to load, save, and print selected sets of key commands

Study the Key Commands window and the Logic terminologies contained therein (often, it helps to cross-reference with the Help files) and then create your own hot list of essential key commands. Carry them with you and commit them to memory.

1. Record	Return
2. Go To Position	G
3. Go To Next Marker	Shift + M
4. Go To Previous Marker	Option + M
5. Mute Region	M
6. Solo Region	S
7. Capture As Recording	Shift + R
8. Record Toggle (drop into play mode)	Command + R
9. Play or Stop	Spacebar
10. Cycle Mode	C
11. Lock/Unlock Current Screenset	Shift + L
12. Show Tools	Escape
13. Next Channel Strip or Plug-In Setting or EXS Instrument	N
14. Previous Channel Strip or Plug-In Setting or EXS Instrument	P
15. Open Color Palette	Option + C
16. Hide/Show Track Automation	A
17. Repeat Regions	R
18. Forward (by one bar)	Right Arrow
19. Rewind (by one bar)	Left Arrow
20. Zoom Horizontal Out	Option + Right Arrow
21. Zoom Horizontal In	Option + Left Arrow
22. Open Key Commands	Option + K
23. Loop Regions	L
24. Convert Loops To Real Copies	Control + L
25. Create Trackname	Shift + N
26. Select Next Track	Down Arrow
27. Select Previous Track	Up Arrow
28. Create Marker	Command + M
29. Toggle Group Clutch	Shift + G
30. Toggle Zoom To Fit Selection (Select All first)	Z

Note: Here's one more essential move worth memorizing: Select a region and then press Ctrl + Shift to disconnect from the beat grid. This lets you slide the region freely along the timeline and it lets you nudge by the smallest increment.

Appendix B: The DVD-ROM Video Tutorials

The accompanying DVD-ROM contains 15 video tutorials to assist you in your pursuit of "Becoming One with Logic." They provide additional insights into some of the tools and techniques covered in the text, along with a real-time glimpse into a creative, efficient Logic workflow.

- Tutorials 1 through 3 cover basic programming in Logic.
- Tutorials 4 through 11 illustrate techniques for manipulating the timing and feel of music that was covered in chapter 9.
- Tutorials 12 through 14 focus on the Marquee tool and how it can help you unlock even more creativity and speed in Logic Pro.

1. Programming Drums

A Logic project is deconstructed to demonstrate the basics of MIDI programming using a factory drum kit in the EXS24 sampler. Quantizing, navigating the Logic transport, MIDI region copying, and aliasing are introduced. The very essential MIDI tool, from the Region Parameter box, is also introduced along with the classic Option-drag tool, which is used for time-compressing MIDI.

2. Programming MIDI with Logic Synths

Several more basic MIDI concepts are covered in this tutorial, including the following:

- Loading and programming with Logic software instruments
- Quantizing
- Viewing notation in real time
- The Capture As Recording feature
- Customizing the Transport and the chain link button to maintain sync between the various Logic editors and windows.

3. Saving Your Project and EXS24 Samples the Right Way

Insights are presented in this tutorial to help you do the following:

- Understand the elements of the Logic project folder
- Avoid the most common mistake Logic users make when saving their projects
- Use the Finder view of the Logic project assets.
- Also covered is Single mode in the Mixer to see, at a glance, the components contained in your project.

4. Making Beats, Part 1: The BPM Plug-in

Discover the Logic metering plug-in for analyzing the tempo of an audio file.

5. Making Beats, Part 2: Time-Stretching Audio

Part 2 provides an introduction to the classic time-stretching tool in Logic, Time-Stretch Region to Locators.

6. Making Beats, Part 3: Option-Drag Time-Stretching

In Making Beats, part 3, we take advantage of the Snap to Absolute Value option in the Snap menu in order to accomplish region-stretching with the Pointer tool.

7. Making Beats, Part 4: Option-Scissors Slicing

In part 4, we cut an audio file by beat, or subdivision of the beat, using the Scissors tool—a classic Logic technique for beat making.

8. Space Designer Warping

This tutorial demonstrates a special use of Logic's convolution reverb to create modern electronic beats with the Warped presets.

9. Flex Audio (Elastic Audio) in Logic, Part 1

An understanding of Flex view and the algorithms used to detect transients is integral to flex editing as well as to the use of special effects that are available via the Tempophone algorithm.

10. Flex Audio, Part 2

Learn the basics of quantizing audio, along with how to implement flex markers to adjust the timing and musical phrasing of an audio performance.

11. Slice At Transient Markers

Become familiar with another tool in Logic for creating variations and breakdowns in your groove. The Slice At Transient Markers option is an extremely valuable tool for slicing and stuttering your beat.

12. Marquee Tool Editing, Part 1: Your Secret Weapon in Logic

The Marquee tool, an essential tool for editing and navigation in Logic, is selected for muting, deleting, and creating independent regions and breakdowns. Discover how to assign it as your Command-click tool.

13. Marquee Tool Editing, Part 2: The Marquee Tool Versus the Scissors Tool

Understand the advantages of selecting the Marquee tool for editing audio and MIDI events.

14. Marquee Tool Editing, Part 3: Single Pixel Playback, Automation Nodes

Part 3 demonstrates two more techniques to improve your workflow in Logic with the Marquee tool: starting playback with the Marquee tool and creating automation nodes.

INDEX

About Dot Bustelo

"When you got a Logic problem
Dot has wrote a book to solve 'em…
And this right hear is it. Yeya!"

—Chad Hugo, *N.E.R.D., The Neptunes*

"Dot Bustelo has been exceptionally helpful in my experience of learning and using Logic. She understands how the artist thinks and always has new tricks to teach."

—A-trak, *DJ/turntablist*

"Dot has made Logic, well, logical. Her approach to teaching is creative and tailored, less from the perspective of a program developer and more so that of a musician and composer."

—Ronnie Vannucci, *The Killers*

"Dot has provided me with an incredible source of in-depth and practical knowledge of Apple's Logic program. She has shown me tricks and tips that have opened creative doors that I didn't even know existed. She has dedicated herself to the absolute mastery of her craft, and is willing to share that wealth of knowledge with the rest of us."

—Nathaniel Motte, *3OH!3*

"Dot Bustelo has hands down the most extensive working knowledge of Logic and all its intricacies; I've asked her questions before, and she's able to mentally scroll through the various menus and folders in her head… leaving me to only assume she and Logic have actually become 'one' entity, which is pretty cool."

—Ryan Tedder, *OneRepublic*

"Dot was the first one to introduce me to Logic software, and she has been a valuable resource of information ever since. She knows this software inside and out, and breaks everything down in an easy-to-understand way. And she knows the best insider techniques that will make your recording more efficient and creative.

Logic is an extremely powerful creative tool, and Dot knows how to get the most out of it. I wonder when Dot will get sick of me asking her Logic-related questions?"

—James Valentine, *Maroon 5*

"My experience with Dot Bustelo and her inspiring Logic tutorials turned me into a Logic user for life. She has a knack for enticing you with her crafty shortcuts that stimulate a deeper understanding….

I have had the pleasure of seeing her perform her demos live…. I always leave feeling excited to get working on my own songs and implement the new tricks, as the logic within Logic takes hold in my own engineering. Dot enchants as she clarifies precisely how to use Logic and has always kept her tutorials fresh and fun. Thank you Dot!"

—DJ Empress

quick PRO guides series

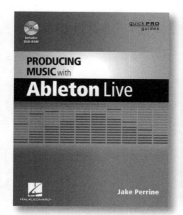

Producing Music with Ableton Live
by Jake Perrine
Softcover w/DVD-ROM •
978-1-4584-0036-9 • $16.99

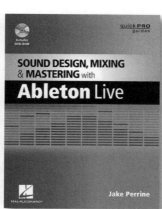

Sound Design, Mixing, and Mastering with Ableton Live
by Jake Perrine
Softcover w/DVD-ROM •
978-1-4584-0037-6 • $16.99

The Power in Reason
by Andrew Eisele
Softcover w/DVD-ROM •
978-1-4584-0228-8 • $16.99

Sound Design and Mixing in Reason
by Andrew Eisele
Softcover w/DVD-ROM •
978-1-4584-0229-5 • $16.99

Mixing and Mastering with Pro Tools
by Glenn Lorbecki
Softcover w/DVD-ROM •
978-1-4584-0033-8 • $16.99

Tracking Instruments and Vocals with Pro Tools
by Glenn Lorbecki
Softcover w/DVD-ROM •
978-1-4584-0034-5 • $16.99

The Power in Logic Pro: Songwriting, Composing, Remixing, and Making Beats
by Dot Bustelo
Softcover w/DVD-ROM •
78-1-4584-1419-9 • $16.99

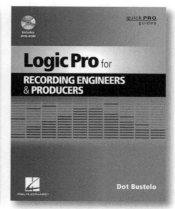

Logic Pro for Recording Engineers and Producers
by Dot Bustelo
Softcover w/DVD-ROM •
978-1-4584-1420-5 • $16.99

The Power in Cubase: Tracking Audio, MIDI, and Virtual Instruments
by Matt Hepworth
Softcover w/DVD-ROM • 978-1-4584-1366-6 • $16.99

Mixing and Mastering with Cubase
by Matt Hepworth
Softcover w/DVD-ROM • 978-1-4584-1367-3 • $16.99

HAL•LEONARD®

Prices, contents, and availability subject to change without notice.

0312